Marketing New Homes

David F. Parker, MIRM
and
Charles R. Clark, MIRM

Home Builder Press®
National Association of Home Builders
1201 15th Street, NW
Washington, DC 20005-2800
(800) 223-2665
www.builderbooks.com

Marketing New Homes

ISBN 0-86718-447-7
New Edition © 1999 by Home Builder Press®
of the National Association of Home Builders
of the United States of America

Cover by David Rhodes, Art and Production Director, Home Builder Press.
Printed in the United States of America.

Library of Congress Cataloging-in-Publication Data

Parker, David F., 1934–
    Marketing new homes / David F. Parker and Charles R. Clark.—New ed.
        p   cm.
    Clark's name appears first on the earlier edition.
    ISBN 0-86718-447-7
    1. Residential real estate—Marketing.   2. House selling.   3. Real estate business.   4. Construction industry—Management.   I. Clark, Charles R., 1930–   . II. Title.
    HD1390.5.C57   1999   98-52745
    333.33'8'0688—dc21   CIP

Disclaimer

This publication is designed to provide accurate and authoritative information in regard to the subject matter covered. It is sold with the understanding that the publisher is not engaged in rendering legal, accounting, or other professional service. If legal advice or other expert assistance is required, the services of a competent professional person should be sought.

—From a declaration of Principles jointly adopted by a committee
of the American Bar Association
and a Committee of Publishers and Associations.

Quantity Discounts
Quantity discounts for individual Home Builder Press titles are available. Multi-title packages are also available for certain books. For further information, please contact—

Director of Marketing
Home Builder Press®
National Association of Home Builders
1201 15th Street, NW
Washington, DC 20005-2800

Check us out online at http://www.builderbooks.com
Or call (800) 368-5242, ext. 394; fax (202) 822-0391

1/99 Harlowe/Kirby Litho 2000

Contents

List of Figures

Acknowledgments

David Parker and Charlie Clark dedicate this book to all of the colleagues, critics, clients, and students who have helped us increase our knowledge of this business over the past four decades. More specifically, we extend special thanks to our many professional associates whose ideas and writing are integrated with our own throughout the book, and to Judy Larrabee, who typed and coordinated the entire text. In addition, we gratefully acknowledge the contributions of the many marketing specialists who graciously permitted us to quote them and use their exhibits in this book.

At the National Association of Home Builders, our thanks to Senior Acquisitions Editor Doris M. Tennyson, who edited and coordinated publication of this book. Thanks also to Meg Meyer, Executive Director of the National Sales and Marketing Council.

Finally, but perhaps most importantly, we are grateful for the patience and love of Marilynn Parker and Trudy Clark, who support our dedication and commitment to improving the art and science of marketing and selling new homes.

Reviewers

Nancie Balun-Boughton, MIRM; CSP; Housing Consultant, Basking Ridge, NJ; Jill Goodwin, Director, Media Relations, National Association of Home Builders; Robert Hankin, RDR Construction Company, Highland Mills, NY; Meg Meyer, Executive Director, National Sales and Marketing Council, National

Association of Home Builders, Washington, D.C.; E. Lee Reid, President, E. Lee Reid and Company, Buena Vista, FL; B. J. Young, MIRM, President, B. J. Young, Inc., Winter Park, FL.

This book was produced under the general direction of Kent Colton, NAHB Executive Vice President and CEO, in association with NAHB staff members James E. Johnson, Jr., Staff Vice President, Information Services Division; Adrienne Ash, Assistant Staff Vice President, Publishing Services; Charlotte McKamy, Publisher; Doris M. Tennyson, Senior Acquisitions Editor; Andrew Schwarz, Director, Sales and Marketing; David Rhodes, Art and Production Director; and Thayer Long, Assistant Editor.

About the Authors

David F. Parker, MIRM, and Charles R. Clark, MIRM, are the authors of *Marketing New Homes* and *Selling New Homes*, both published by the National Association of Home Builders in 1989 when the authors were principals of Clark Parker Associates, Inc., an international real estate marketing and sales consultant organization. In 1990 they formed separate consultant firms. (Both books are now out of print.)

David F. Parker is president of Parker Associates, real estate development/marketing consultants in Jacksonville, Florida. During his career he has been responsible for a wide range of management, development, and marketing innovations spanning both public and private development of real estate on three continents. He has been a chief executive of development and building companies in addition to serving as planner, researcher, teacher, and consultant. Dr. Parker is the recipient of several design and marketing awards and has authored many articles and reports on marketing, planning, budgeting, and management.

Charles R. Clark, MIRM, is principal of Charles R. Clark Company in Ponte Vedra, Florida. He is known by builders, Realtors®, and lenders throughout the United States and Britain for his educational and motivational seminars on marketing and selling new homes as well as his marketing advisory services. He is a past president of the Institute of Residential Marketing, a founding trustee of the prestigious National Society of Builder Marketing Specialists, and past chairman of the National Sales and Marketing Council of the National Association of Home Builders. He has served as a lecturer for the NAHB Regional Leadership Training Conferences and as a featured speaker at the annual conventions of the National Association of Realtors®. Clark was the recipient of the prestigious William Molster award in 1991.

Introduction

The purpose of this book is to provide a concise guide to understanding new and changing markets and marketing methods for home builders who want to expand their businesses. If you currently build or plan to build 25 or more homes annually and you are committed to increasing your sales revenues each year, you should find this book especially helpful.

Marketing New Homes provides entirely new information on (a) emerging consumer groups, (b) the efficient use of computers to support your marketing program, and (c) how to create a competitive advantage over other builders through cost-effective marketing procedures. The guidelines in this book build upon the strong foundation for marketing originally presented in our first marketing book by the same name, *Marketing New Homes* (published by Home Builder Press in 1989 and now out of print). Our updated guidelines focus on helping builders improve their in-house marketing and on obtaining effective results from outside marketing specialists.

Since writing our first book 10 years ago in the free-spending 1980s, a number of new trends have emerged in new home consumers as well as in the homebuilding business. The surge of new home consumers in the 1980s was the baby-boom generation born in the 1940s and 1950s who learned extravagant spending habits from their parents' purchasing splurge on the vast array of new products in the postwar economy. Consumer debt rose to record levels in the 1980s and the homebuilding business kept pace, until the overheated economy collapsed into recession at the beginning of the 1990s.

The 1991 national economic recession generated latent demand for housing, but the new home consumers of this decade proved to be more demanding and knowledgeable than the consumers of the 1980s. Lending institutions dramatically declined in number with the collapse of savings and loan lenders, and they became even more demanding than new home consumers. Market research for proposed residential developments became a necessity rather than a special purpose requirement and home builders began learning about the psychographic characteristics of consumers, the role of electronics in the home, targeted amenity packages, and pricing segmentation. The entire homebuilding industry attained a new plateau of understanding about the design and marketing of new home products to increasingly sophisticated consumers.

In the first decade of the new millenium, the rapid changes of the 1990s are likely to intensify. Baby boomers will be older and more affluent, but their children will be establishing their own households and consequently creating the largest number of empty nesters and emergent retirees in history. The building industry will become increasingly competitive and necessitate greater emphasis on consumer targeting, distinctive design, and cost-effective marketing. The contents of this book will help you capitalize on these changes.

This book is designed to provide readers with ready-to-use procedures for all aspects of new homes marketing in the new century. The procedures are organized into a three-phase marketing system that provides a step-by-step recipe for increasing your flow of qualified prospects.

The New Marketing System

The new homes marketing system described in this book was developed over many years of marketing new homes. It provides basic procedures that have succeeded in the 1990s and can be applied to the changes identified for the future. The basic procedures have been tested by hundreds of builders across the United States and in other countries. New ideas were selected for their potential positive impact on these proven procedures.

Figure I-1 on the next page illustrates the 12 components of the New Homes Marketing System. They are organized into three phases—*Manage, Market, Monitor*—the three Ms of new homes marketing. The following paragraphs summarize the three Ms.

Manage

Effective new homes marketing requires a plan and budget based upon carefully designed new product offerings positioned according to accurate information about the market. You must assemble and coordinate a team of marketing specialists to carry out the plan. These management functions are essential to a continuing and expanding marketing program.

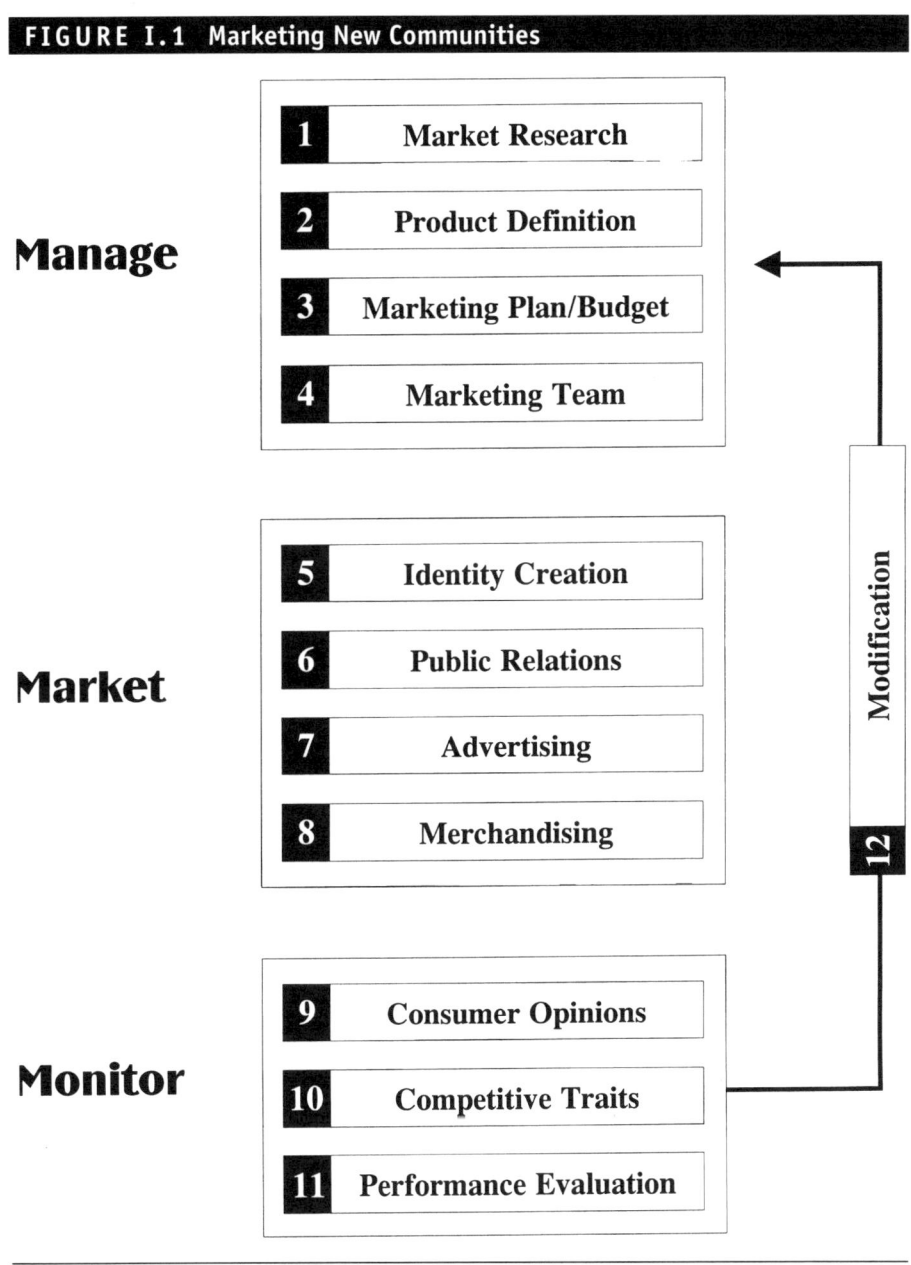

FIGURE I.1 Marketing New Communities

Manage
1 Market Research
2 Product Definition
3 Marketing Plan/Budget
4 Marketing Team

Market
5 Identity Creation
6 Public Relations
7 Advertising
8 Merchandising

Monitor
9 Consumer Opinions
10 Competitive Traits
11 Performance Evaluation

12 Modification

1. Market Research includes the collection and analysis of accurate and consistent information about consumers and competition. Intuition and creativity are valuable, but they must be guided by hard facts about consumer characteristics, needs, preferences, and financial capabilities plus comparative data on the performance of your competition. This information determines the best types of dwellings and amenities for consumer groups with high potential for being converted into new home purchasers. It also provides pricing and sales absorption guidelines for preparing the marketing plan and budget.

2. Product Definition translates the results of research on consumer preferences and competition performance into homes of specific types, designs, prices, benefits, and features as well as related community amenities to define new home products in terms of specific benefits to targeted consumer groups.

3. Marketing Plan and Budget provides annual marketing activities necessary to attract consumers and support the sales process along with estimated costs of these activities. The plan and budget extends through the sellout of a specific development and/or through one or more years in the future for a multi-site builder operation.

4. Marketing Team includes all staff and outside consultants responsible for the marketing program. You must decide which functions can be performed by in-house staff and which require outside consultants. This system requires you to establish selection criteria for choosing specialists for such functions as public relations, advertising, and merchandising. You also need coordination policies to ensure the cost-effective functioning of the team.

Market

The Market phase implements the marketing plan defined under the Manage phase according to plan objectives. You would describe these objectives in terms of number of consumer inquiries, conversion rate of inquiries to sales, and net sales. For example, if the sales objective is 10 and the sales staff conversion rate is 5 percent (10 divided by .05), 200 new inquiries are required to meet the sales objective.

The Manage phase defines the marketing objectives, the program actions, and the team responsibilities for achieving them. The Market phase coordinates the four components of marketing described below.

5. Identity Creation is the essential first step in marketing implementation. It includes names, logo, and colors that are to be used consistently in stationery and advertising as well as signs, brochures, and other collateral materials.

6. Public Relations includes publicity, direct communications, community involvement, and promotions that enhance the builder's image among key segments of the marketplace, including consumers, financial executives, government officials, and real estate agents.

7. Advertising must identify cost-effective communications media and develop a creative strategy to present the builder's homes and communities in appealing fashion.

8. Merchandising supports the sales process by creating an attractive presentation of the product from the moment the potential purchaser first arrives at the community through the visit to the information center and a tour of the model home(s). Community merchandising elements include landscaping, entry, directional and identification signs, and the information center exterior and interior. Model merchandising enhances the dwelling interior through the creative use of color, light, fabric, textures, furniture placement, and accessories.

Monitor

Marketing is continually improved through the three elements of the Monitor phase. These elements are transformed into recommendations for change and information for the Manage phase.

9. Consumer Opinions about your product offerings and marketing methods provide the best information for improving your business. You can obtain their opinions through various types of primary (person-to-person) market research techniques described in this book.

10. Competitive Traits of other builders' products must be reviewed on a regular basis to compare your offerings and sales process with the competition. You can gather them by having sales representatives use standard forms or purchase forms from consultant services.

11. Performance Evaluation is essential and should be conducted on a regular schedule using input from the preceding two components in addition to sales representative's comments about the performance of products, marketing, and sales procedures.

12. Modification recommendations from regular product performance evaluations provide management guidance for revisions to products and marketing in a continuing cycle of system improvement.

I

MANAGE

Successful management of marketing requires a builder or sales manager to—

- project feasible pricing and sales absorption rates (rate of sales per month or year) upon which to base marketing decisions.
- objective selection of sites, lots, and dwelling types
- a strategic marketing plan designed to attract specific types of new home consumers and to impress them with a presentation on the new homes and neighborhood that is designed expressly for them

1

Projecting Marketing Feasibility

Traditionally home builders were taught that success followed a simple formula of constructing a quality home in a neighborhood of similar homes. However, American cities, towns, and neighborhoods have grown increasingly complex. American consumers are also more knowledgeable about the homebuilding process and more demanding about fulfilling their ideal lifestyle requirements. The issues of what to build and where to build it are no longer simple. The successful builder decides these issues through a sophisticated management process that plans for each new development site in advance of finalizing acquisition.

In a 1991 survey by the NAHB Builders Economic Council, only half of the respondent builders always undertook market research before starting—67 percent of large-volume builders and 39 percent of small-volume builders. Builder size and applied market research appeared to have a direct correlation.

Charles A. Brown, Jr., retired president of Summerhomes, Inc., in Jacksonville, Florida, reports that his firm's growth relied strongly on analyzing marketing feasibility prior to purchasing new building lots or development sites. From its inception in 1976, Summerhomes expanded rapidly to become one of the major builders in the Jacksonville market, averaging 200 to 300 new homes per year from 1983 to 1994 before its termination upon Brown's retirement.

In selecting a new development site, each builder must ensure that projected profit and return on investment meet business objectives. Meeting business objectives first requires analyzing the market in terms of consumer demand and product competition. New home offerings at this location should be designed and marketed to take advantage of consumer preferences that are not being satisfied by competitive products. This competitive advantage allows you to forecast annual revenues with confidence.

The method of projecting marketing feasibility relies upon your understanding of consumer demand and product competition. This understanding is the basis for pricing and annual sales projections of new homes designed to satisfy unfulfilled consumer demand. The result yields annual revenues which, when combined with cost estimates, provide development financial feasibility defined as profit and return on investment. These steps are illustrated in Figure 1.1.

Understanding market area consumers and their needs and preferences is described below followed by the process of identifying competitive new home product offerings. These two sets of information provide the foundation for new home product definition and revenues projection.

Know Your Consumer

Small-volume builders often know each of their purchasers personally. They can project with reasonable accuracy the characteristics and preferences of future purchasers by their knowledge of past purchasers. But annual sales growth makes getting to know each of your purchasers increasingly difficult. And expansion means diversifying your products to attract new types of consumers. Numbers

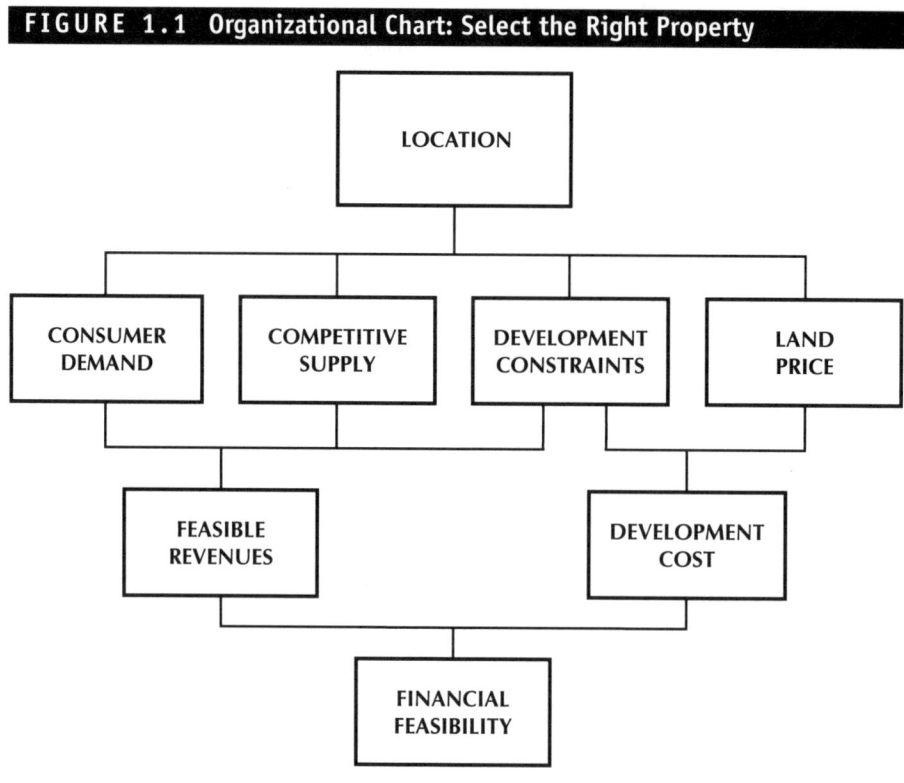

FIGURE 1.1 Organizational Chart: Select the Right Property

tend to replace names, and broad categories such as move-up buyer and empty nester couple replace personal household characteristics.

As stated by Engle Homes V. P. Mike Moore, "our Dallas-Fort Worth consumers expect to have new homes designed to match their particular preferences . . . we must understand the predominant consumer preferences in a particular area and price range prior to planning new homes in that area."

New home consumer groups are changing in terms of location preferences, household composition, predominant age range, levels of income, values, and lifestyle. Marketing methods of the 1980s are not cost-effective in the 1990s and will be wasteful in the 21st century.

Builders must identify and communicate with specific groups of consumers who exhibit distinctive needs and preferences. Success means knowing your consumers, designing products just for them, and targeting communications directly to them.

The following information summarizes methods of defining consumer target groups relevant to marketing new homes. It provides an overview of available consumer knowledge, some of which you may wish to explore to gain a competitive advantage over other builders in your marketplace.

Geographic Market Definition

Geographic definition is one of the simplest methods of dividing areas into possible markets: where people live, work, and play. Geographic markets can be national, regional, or local, the latter comprising a metropolitan area, county, city, township, zip code, census tract, or neighborhood. Many builders are concerned only with local market area definition.

The United States Bureau of the Census provides population characteristics for all political jurisdictions in this country composed of census tracts and subtracts (block groups). Most builders are aware of local, city, and metropolitan area population trends and projections. These data are readily available from local government planning offices and libraries at little or no cost.

The U.S. Census provides population data by geographic area in the Topologically Integrated Geographic Encoding and Referencing (TIGER) system, which provides computer-readable mapping and a geographic data base for the entire nation. Because the TIGER files require relatively sophisticated computer processing, most end-users purchase specific types of data from the several dozen data service vendors that provide TIGER-related services including computer mapping. Your local planning office probably purchases such data for small area population projections.

In addition to census tracts and political jurisdictions (including metropolitan areas), data service vendors can provide population characteristics in other configurations including zip codes and geometric study areas, such as rings of specified radiuses around an identified site or address preferred by retail developers. Other geometric shapes—bands, sectors, polygons—are available through arithmetic apportionment of census tracts. These data can be purchased for modest fees from data service providers listed at the end of this book.

Special geographic designations have become well-known for certain purposes, such as the area of dominant influence (ADI), usually consisting of one or more counties, defined by the Arbitron Company for media ratings; A. C. Nielson uses designated market area (DMA) for a similar purpose.

People, Jobs, and Social Class

Demography is the statistical study of human populations, often referred to as geodemographics when population data are organized by geographic area. Socioeconomic factors examine a population in terms of economic and social classes. This term demographics is frequently used to include both demographic and socioeconomic factors. Demographic factors include population, age distribution, marital status, household/family size, gender, race, nationality, and religion. Socioeconomic factors include education, occupation, income, social class, and dwelling type.

The primary demographic factors describe the scale of the market: population, households, household size. For residential developers and builders, households and their size are essential components for market analysis to define new home plans. Figure 1.2 summarizes nationwide household trends and projections indicating the proportions of older-person households and declining family households.

Age classification defines persons in various age groups or life stages who exhibit similarities in purchase behavior. For example, first-time home purchasers tend to be adults under age 35, a declining age group in the 1990s.

Figure 1.3 illustrates the changing character of the national population by age classification. In 1970, 28 percent of the population was under 15 years of age and less than 10 percent was over age 65, whereas in 2010 only about 20 percent will be under age 15, and 14 percent will be over 65. The entire population continues to age.

FIGURE 1.2 Household Trends

	Young Singles & Couples (no kids) < Age 45		Older Singles & Couples (no kids) Age 45 >		Families With Kids All Ages
1990	19%		41%		40%
2010	17%		48%		35%

2000 New Home Demand

	Young Singles & Couples		Older Singles & Couples		Families With Kids	
Multi	15%		10%		7%	34%
Single	10%		23%		30%	66%

Marital status provides essential data for planning residential developments, particularly as the number of traditional families with children continues to decline and single-person and single-parent households increase. This trend varies substantially from market to market, so be certain to rely on local rather than national projections for planning new developments.

Although federal law prohibits discrimination in housing, the fact is that new home and neighborhood design and marketing require various approaches for consumers with different ethnic backgrounds, countries of national origin, and religious preferences. Current demographic projections indicate that minorities represent the majority of all growth for the foreseeable future. For example, in southern California, Texas, and Florida, builders design new homes for extended families of Latin-American origin; sales persons must speak both Spanish and English. This trend toward multicultural differentiation will continue in the future as national immigration generates increasing numbers of Asian and Latin-American communities in addition to those of other origins already established throughout the country.

In terms of socioeconomic factors, most observers realize a strong relationship exists between educational background, occupation, and income. Home ownership also is related to these factors with ownership rising in accordance with higher education, occupation, and income achievement.

Economics and Employment

Occupation related to the economy of a market area usually is reflected in industry growth trends and employment. Thus, job growth usually provides an indicator of new home demand. Employment trends divided by population trends in a market area indicate short-term future growth. Some housing economists prefer to divide employment by housing permits to provide a similar indicator of short-term future housing demand. This ratio must be tempered by changing numbers of dual income households in the local market being examined.

For example, employment growth in the services industry during the 1990s in a Florida two-county market area surged. This surge translates into potential increasing housing demand for increasing numbers of modest-income services employees. It is caused by a growing retiree market that generates a high demand for services. It should be accompanied by a declining rate of unemployment unless publicity about the economic growth attracts more immigrants seeking employment than it attracts new jobs.

Local markets in northern states are unlikely to exhibit such pronounced employment changes unless a major employer relocates in the area. Lexington, Kentucky, experienced such a change in the 1980s when Toyota established a plant north of the city. The housing market subsequently experienced rapid changes in overall demand as well as a disproportionate increase in demand for modest-priced family homes.

Social Clustering

Social class is more difficult to define than the census-based data described above, but it provides vital consumer purchasing characteristics for market analysis. Over

FIGURE 1.3 U.S. Population: Age Demographics

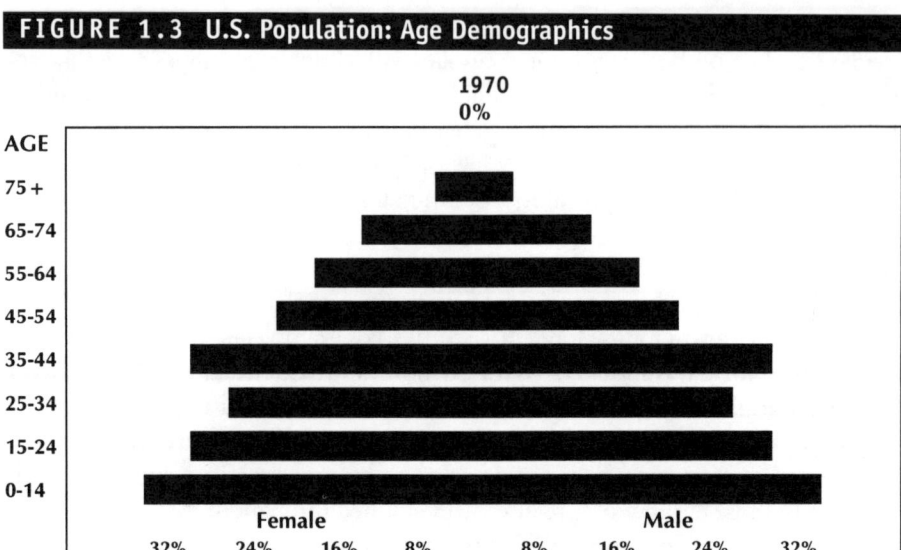

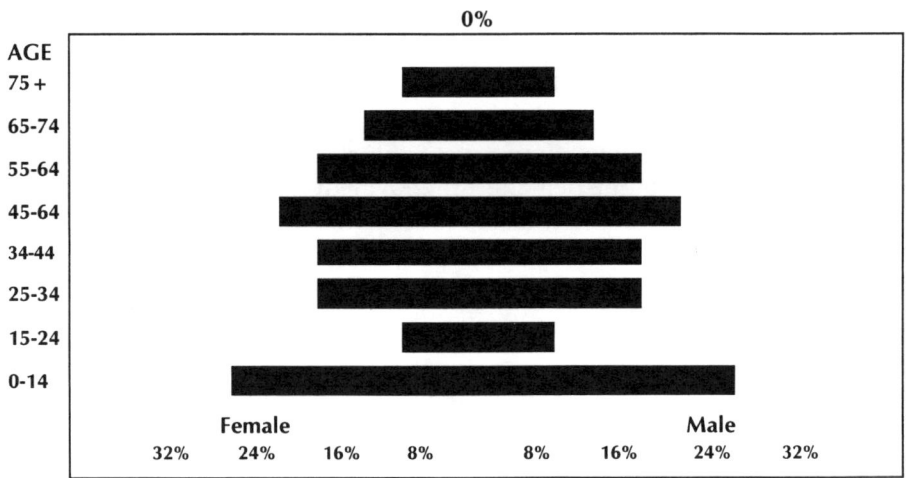

the past 20 years, cluster-based geodemographic systems have been developed to identify neighborhoods by social class on the now-proven premise that persons of like characteristics tend to cluster into neighborhood groupings. Census-based data systems such as Donnelley's Cluster-Plus, Clarita's PRIZM, and CACI's ACORN provide detailed insight about American neighborhoods (see Appendix B). According to Donnelley, knowing in which cluster a consumer lives provides a reasonable means of understanding how that consumer will behave in the marketplace.

Americans always have preferred to live in proximity with neighbors of their own social and economic group. The 1962 advent of the U.S. Postal Service's Zone Improvement Plan, known as the zip code, made possible the collection of resident data by neighborhood pioneered by Jonathan Robbin in the 1970s. Robbin matched zip codes with census data and consumer surveys in a target-marketing system he called PRIZM (Potential Rating Index for ZIP Markets) which originally sorted the nation's 36,000 zip codes into 40 "lifestyle clusters" with characteristic names such as Blue Blood Estates, Money and Brains, Furs and Station Wagons, and Young Suburbia.

Figure 1.4 summarizes some key characteristics of Claritas's Young Suburbia. You can use these characteristics to target specific products to residents of neighborhoods most receptive to these products. In marketing new homes, neighborhoods of targeted consumers can be contacted directly as a supplement or alternative to media advertising.

Clarita's Cluster Group 16, Big Fish, Small Ponds, included 77 percent of a census tract in a city targeted for move-up new home prospects. The general characteristics of this cluster group are white married couples age 35 to 54 with some college education, children, and white-collar employment, who live in single-family detached homes. Specific demographic characteristics of residents in this census tract compared to the national profile of similar cluster groups is shown in Figure 1.5. It provides an excellent information base for planning target marketing aimed at the residents of this neighborhood.

Consumer Values and Lifestyle

The foregoing demographic definition provides qualitative understanding of consumers' leisure-time activities, interests, and opinions. The means of defining these lifestyle characteristics in combination with demographic characteristics have become known as *psychographics*; they are techniques to understand the underlying emotions of individual purchase decisions. The word *psychographics* is derived from combining psychology and demographics. It includes relationships among the four groups of lifestyle characteristics summarized in Figure 1.6.

Although detailed knowledge of consumer values and lifestyles may not be necessary to every builder's success, a basic understanding will help you know your consumers better. The more you know about them, the better your decisions on product design and marketing expenditures will be.

FIGURE 1.4 Young Suburbia: Key Characteristics

PRIZM Cluster ZQ8 of 50 Neighborhoods Clusters Defined by Claritas Corporation

Demographics	Lifestyle
5.3% of US Households	Swimming Pools
Primary Age Range: 25–44	Mutual Funds
Median Household Income: $48,875	Health Clubs
Median Home Value: $118,166	Racquetball
Single-Family Homes	Home Computers
College Education	Foreign Tour Packages
White-Collar Jobs	

FIGURE 1.5 Southern City Census Tract

Race/Ancestry	Cluster	U.S.	Occupation	Cluster	U.S.
White	94.7	83.2	Professional/Mgr.	30.2	26.6
Black	2.8	12.4	Other White Collar	32.4	31.8
All Other Races	2.4	4.4	Blue Collar	24.9	26.1
Hispanic	3.8	9.9	Service	10.6	13.1
Asian Ancestry	3.2	5.4	Farming/Mining/ Ranching	1.9	2.4

Household Income	Cluster	U.S.	Family Type	Cluster	U.S.
Less than $25,000	21.2	36.5	Married Couples	33.6	28.1
$25–34,999	34.6	32.6	Married Couples/ Children	34.7	26.6
$50–74,999	37.0	26.0			
$100,000+	7.0	6.2	Single Parents	6.1	9.1
			Single (Not Married)	25.7	36.2

Home Value	Cluster	U.S.	Presence of Children	Cluster	U.S.
Less than $50,000	5.9	21.1	Under age 6	9.1	9.2
$50–100,000	42.6	36.6	Age 6 to 13	12.6	11.6
$100–150,000	28.4	17.7	Age 13 to 17	5.6	5.1
$150–250,000	17.4	15.1	HH w/5 + Persons	10.8	10.8
$250,000+	5.7	9.6			
Median Home Value	**$106,400**	**$106,800**			

			Age of Population	Cluster	U.S.
Education	Cluster	U.S.	Under 24	8.1	10.1
4+ Years College	23.9	20.5	25 to 44	23.7	32.0
1–3 Year College	29.2	25.1	45 to 64	13.3	20.2
High School Graduate	31.1	29.9	65 +	10.4	12.7
Less than 8th Grade	5.5	10.2	**Median Age**	**45.2**	**46.5**

FIGURE 1.6 Lifestyle Characteristics

Activities	Interests	Opinions	Demographics
Work	Family	Themselves	Age
Hobbies	Home	Social Issues	Education
Social Events	Job	Politics	Income
Vacations	Community	Business	Occupation
Entertainment	Recreation	Economic	Family Size
Club Membership	Fashion	Education	Dwelling
Community	Food	Products	Geographic
Shopping	Media	Future	City Size
Sports	Achievements	Culture	Stage of Life

The first and most widely accepted psychographics system is the Values and Lifestyles (VALS™) System of SRI Consulting, subsidiary of SRI International. The original VALS System, introduced in 1978, grouped Americans into nine categories based on clusters of shared values and beliefs (social attitude statements.) After a decade of use by marketing professionals, VALS was replaced in 1989 with VALS 2 which categorizes U.S. adults into eight consumer segments based on psychological characteristics selected for their correlation with consumer purchasing behavior.

As illustrated in Figure 1.7, the eight VALS consumer segments are organized in a rectangular framework arranged vertically by resources (education, incomes, self-confidence, health, eagerness to buy) and horizontally by three self-orientations: principle, status, and action. The segments each range from10 to 17 percent of the U.S. population. Actualizers and strugglers are not included in the horizontal self-orientation categories.

Although full application of VALS research may be beyond the budgets of most builders, an understanding of the principles of this categorization is essential to cost-effective marketing. For example, a community designed expressly for Achievers is likely to have negative appeal for Fulfilleds. Achievers are status-oriented consumers seeking a secure place in a valued social setting; that is, they base their purchase decisions on factors that demonstrate their success to their peers. They are more likely to be attracted by an obviously expensive community entrance with fully staffed gatehouse and lavish landscaping (Figure 1.8) than Fulfilleds. Fulfilleds are principle-oriented consumers who demand functionality, value, and durability in their products. They tend to view the community entrance in Figure 1.8 as unnecessarily expensive and assume that the cost would

FIGURE 1.7 VALS™ Consumer Type

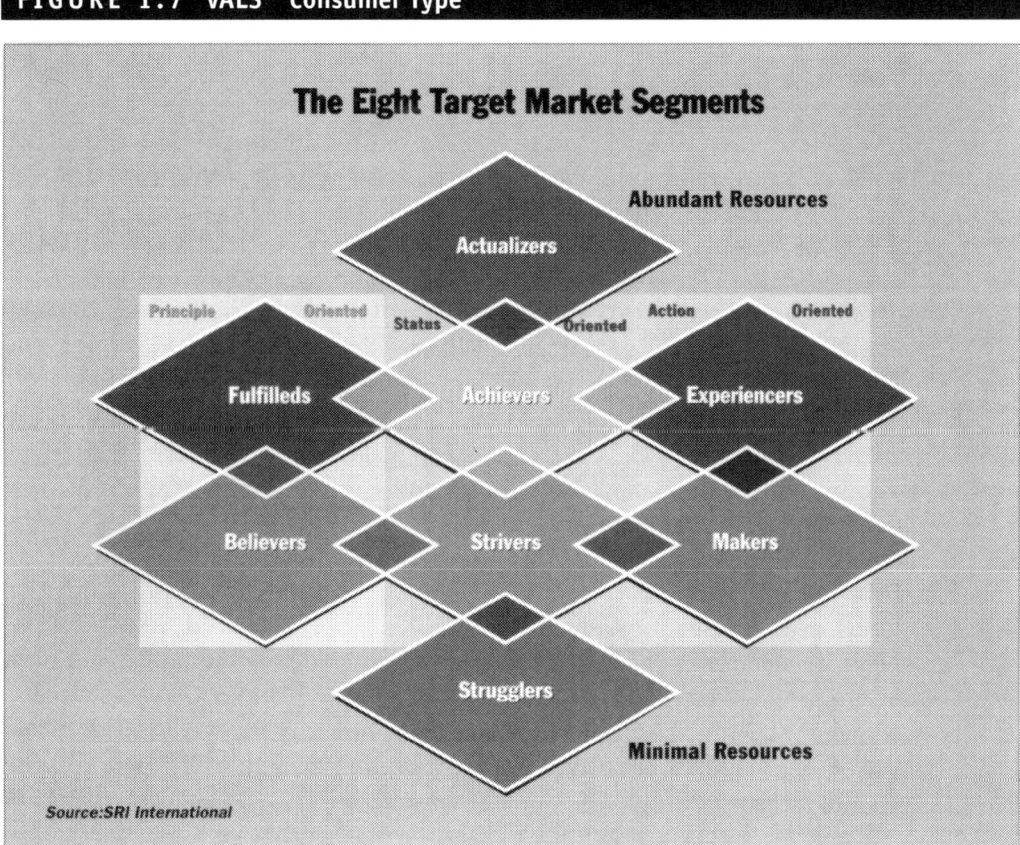

The Eight Target Market Segments

Source:SRI International

Note: VALS™ is a registered trademark of SRI International, Menlo Park California.

FIGURE 1.8 Community Gate and Landscaping

Courtesy of Queens Harbour Yacht and Country Club, Jacksonville, Florida.

be reflected in lot prices of less than good value. Therefore the developer and builders of this community would be advised to target Achievers and not waste money attempting to attract Fulfilleds.

Achievers are increasing nationwide relative to other psychographic VALS groups because of the growing affluence and conspicuous consumption of the huge population segment born between 1940 and 1960 who were raised by generally extravagant parents. These Achievers will enter long retirement years in the new millenium and generate demand for new types of communities and housing.

Several other psychographics systems have been developed for advertising research, including D. D. B. Needham's Life Style Study, N. W. Ayer's The Power Group, and Grey Advertising's Households of the 1990s: America's New Grownups, as well as psychographic systems for international marketing.

Information Sources

Geographic information about your local market area is available from local and regional government planning agencies. Detailed demographic data on both historic and projected future trends are published in planning reports as well as chamber of commerce and economic development agency publications. The source of these data usually is a state planning agency or designated state research organization often located in a state university. Reports usually are available for purchase at a modest charge. Other sources include several publications and computer services of the U.S. Bureau of the Census, including the annual U.S. Statistical Abstract, as well as several national demographics providers such as CACI Marketing Systems, Claritas, Donnelly, National Decision Systems, SRDS, and Woods and Poole. *American Demographics* monthly magazine is the leading source for a wide range of demographic information on trends and analysis of data.

Social class is defined according to neighborhood cluster groupings by CACI, Claritas, Donnelly, and SRDS, as well as a number of smaller service organizations. VALS developed its own geographic location system called GeoVALS. Each offers data by computer modem and fax as well as by mail. Costs vary by the amount and categories of data requested. VALS information is available directly from its creator, SRI Consulting. In addition, SRI has joint-venture agreements with Simmons. *The Yankelovitch Monitor* is an annual review of more than 50 social trends. The *List of Values* from the University of Michigan assesses dominant values within individuals. Other services include DYG's Environmental Scanning Program, D. D. B. Needham's Life Style Study, Ogilvy and Mather's New Wave, and Backer Spielvogel Bates Worldwide's Global Scan.

The above-listed descriptions of information about consumers is purposely brief. It is intended to provide you an overview of available information to facilitate your general understanding of consumer research potential. More detailed knowledge can be attained from the sources listed in Appendix B, many of which are available at no charge in your local public library.

Consumer Survey Techniques

You can obtain information on consumer needs and preferences by asking questions through surveys of householders and new homes sales persons by mail, telephone, e-mail, and personal interview. Consumer focus groups and development-team brainstorming on specific design and marketing issues also can produce valuable marketing information. Each should be designed to meet the following requirements:

- clearly stated response objectives
- a plan for securing reliable answers from a representative sample of respondents whether the data are collected from interviews, group discussion, or survey questionnaires
- specific questions to be answered or information required
- appropriate questionnaire format, including types of questions (for example: multiple choice, open-ended questions, scaling, and/or ranking alternatives)
- strategic question sequencing
- a maximum of 20 questions for telephone and mail surveys and 30 questions for personal interview surveys

Consumer Opinion Surveys

The traditional consumer opinion survey provides a quantitative sampling of consumer answers to specific questions about a particular product or subject. The questions are asked by mail, telephone, or in person with response rates increasing in accordance with personal contact. Incentives also can be offered to increase response, such as a gift or donation to charity for participation.

Survey responses customarily are entered into computer programs designed for this purpose. These programs provide a summary of answers in numeric, percentage, and graphic format. They also provide cross-tabulation of answers, for example, 69 percent of survey respondents prefer white kitchen cabinets, and of those who prefer white cabinets, 85 percent have incomes above $75,000, and 74 percent are age 35 to 55. New advances in computer technology have decreased the cost and increased the speed of achieving survey results.

For example, a builder surveyed new homeowners in suburban Atlanta neighborhoods near a proposed development of similar new home products. Questioned about the need for amenities and assuming the amenities in question would add to the cost of their homes and to their annual association fees, 15 percent of the consumers responded that they would choose no amenities.

Visitor Exit Surveys

An economical means of learning the characteristics of potential consumers is to question visitors departing your model home or information center. This type of survey must be brief and the questions not too intensive in terms of preferences, but you can learn about their opinions of your community, models, and sales presentation. Inexperienced but pleasant persons on a modest fee per completed survey can conduct these surveys. Figure 1.9 provides a sample of an exit survey questionnaire.

New Owner Surveys

Many builders survey their new homeowners two or even three times after move-in to learn about their satisfaction with their purchase and the builder's staff as well as to stimulate referrals of prospects. From new owner surveys you can gain valuable insights into—

- housing needs
- levels of satisfaction
- product features and designs
- marketing effectiveness
- sales presentation performance

Their opinions are particularly valuable within 30 to 45 days after purchase. A second follow-up survey conducted about a year after purchase provides a useful comparison with the initial follow-up survey, particularly if the second questionnaire emanates from an independent source, such as a market research company. Thus, the new owner follow-up survey has dual purposes: (a) it informs the new resident that you are vitally interested in purchaser satisfaction as well as opinions, and (b) it collects facts and opinions for your management information and application.

The second survey's primary purpose is collecting independent opinions from the residents without bias from those who might like to communicate directly with you on complaints or other issues.

Survey Design. Both of these surveys should be designed by professionals in accordance with the particular needs and circumstances of each builder. However, the

FIGURE 1.9 Sample Exit Survey

Community Name: _____   Date: _____

Thank you for visiting our community. We would appreciate your response to the following questions to help us improve our reception and community for future visitors. (Survey should require only three minutes)

1   How long have you been looking for a new home (in this market)?   [   ] Months

2   Are you working with a realtor?   yes [   ]   no [   ]

3   During your search, which communities would you rate the best (besides this one)?

Please list: 1   _____

               2   _____

               3   _____

               4   _____

4   We would like your opinion on how this communitiy rates compared to your number one selection above?
Please give us your impressions of our:
(Please be absolutely honest with us!!)

	1	2	3	4	5
	Superior <---- ---Average--- ---->				Worst
1 Community Location					
2 Appeal of Exterior Elevations					
3 Interior Floorplans					
4 Dwelling Standard Features					
5 Construction Quality					
6 New Home Value					
7 Community Amenities					

5   Was the sales professional who assisted you :

	1	2	3	4	5
	Superior <---- ---Average--- ---->				Worst
1 Enthusiastic and cheerful?					
2 Polite and well-groomed?					
3 Interested in you and your housing needs?					
4 Knowledgeable about all aspects of the community and dwellings?					
5 Successful in providing a clear and well organized presentation of the community?					

6   Currently are you an owner or a renter?   Homeowner [   ]   Renter [   ]

7   What is the ZIP Code of present home?   ___ ___ ___ ___ ___

8   How many people in your household fall into the following age groups?

Children under 18 years   [   ]   Adults 50 to 64 years   [   ]
Adults 18 to 34 years   Adults 65 years or more
Adults 35 to 49 years

9   How could this community and/or homes be improved?

_____

_____

Your opinions are very important to us. Thank you for your time!

FIGURE 1.10 Homeowner Survey

Jacksonville Homeowner Survey SH

Subdivision _____ Address _____

Hello! I'm _____, a student here in Jacksonville. We are conducting a survey for Parker Consumer Research to find out people's attitudes about where they choose to live. We would very much like to have your opinions.

1. Do you own or rent this home?   Own ❑   Rent ❑

2. Did you purchase it new?   Yes ❑   No ❑

3. When did you purchase it? (close on your home)   Month _____ Year_____

4. What was the ZIP code of your previous home?   Zip _____

5. What size is your home?   Bedrooms_____ Bathrooms_____ Square Feet_____

6. What size is your lot?   Feet _____ × _____

7. What was the approximate purchase price?

Under $100,000 ❑	$140–150,000 ❑
$100–110,000 ❑	$150–160,000 ❑
$110–120,000 ❑	$160–170,000 ❑
$120–130,000 ❑	Over $180,000 ❑

8. Who is the builder? _____

9. Which design factor was most important in selecting your home (choose 1)

Floor Plan ❑	Interior Appearance ❑
Quality Construction ❑	Other_____ ❑
Exterior Appearance ❑	

10. What was the most important factor in your decision to purchase? (choose 1)

Builder Reputation ❑	Community Amenities ❑
Home Value ❑	Community Location ❑
Home Price ❑	Other_____ ❑

11.   If community recreation amenities (e.g. pool, tennis, picnic shelter) add to the home price and mean higher association fees, would you prefer . . .

Full Recreation Amenities (Security, Clubhouse, Pool, Tennis, Playground, Basketball) ❑
Reduced Recreation Amenities (Cabana, Small Pool, Playground) ❑
No Recreation Amenities ❑

12. If a security gate or 24-hour security service would add to your monthly association fees would you consider this a valuable service?   Yes ❑   No ❑

13. Would an increased drive time to stores, restaurants and commercial centers preclude you from taking advantage of a better home value?   Yes ❑   No ❑

14. What are your household's favorite recreation activities?

(1 _____ (2 _____ (3 _____

15. How did you first learn about this home or community?

Newspaper Ad ❑	Magazine Ad ❑	Billboard ❑
Radio/TV ❑	Real Estate Agent ❑	Friend ❑ Other _____ ❑

continued

FIGURE 1.10 Continued

16. What do you like best about your home? _____

17. What would you change if you could do it over again?_____

_____

18. What do you like best about this community (neighborhood)?_____

_____

19. Is there anything that could be improved that would make it a better community? _____

_____

20. In what type of home did you live before moving into you current home?

A single detached home on a standard lot ❑	A condominium ❑
A patio home ❑	An apartment ❑
A townhouse ❑	Other_____ ❑

22. Did you: Own ❑   Live with friends/family ❑
              Rent ❑   Other_____ ❑

23. What is your marital status?   Single ❑ Married ❑ Separated ❑ Divorced ❑ Widowed ❑

24. How many people live in your household? _____

25. How many are (write #):   Children under 6____   13–18 ____

                                6–12 ____   children over 18 ____

26. How many wage earners are there? ____

27. What are their ages?
    1st Wage Earner   Under 25 ❑   25–34 ❑   35–44 ❑   45–54 ❑   55–64 ❑   65 or over ❑
    2nd Wage Earner   Under 25 ❑   25–34 ❑   35–44 ❑   45–54 ❑   55–64 ❑   65 or over ❑

28. What was their last year of formal education?
    1st Wage Earner   Some High School ❑   High School Grad. ❑   Some College ❑
                       College Grad ❑   Post-Grad. ❑
    2nd Wage Earner   Some High School ❑   High School Grad. ❑   Some College ❑
                       College Grad ❑   Post-Grad. ❑

29. What is Their Occupation?
    1st   Wage EarnerProfessional/Managerial ❑ Technical/Sales ❑ Service ❑ Production/Repair ❑
    Other ❑
    2nd   Wage EarnerProfessional/Managerial ❑ Technical/Sales ❑ Service ❑ Production/Repair ❑
    Other ❑

30. How far does each commute to work?   1st Wage Earner ____ 2nd Wage Earner ____ Miles

    What is work ZIP code?   1st Wage Earner _____   2nd Wage Earner _____

31. What is your approximate household income?
Under $40,000 ❑	in the $50s ❑	in the $70s ❑	in the $90s ❑
in the $40s ❑	in the $60s ❑	in the $80s ❑	Over $90 ❑

Thank you for your cooperation!

initial design can normally be used for several years of questioning. Figure 1.10 presents a successful homeowner survey.

Surveying Procedures. Once you have surveys designed for both the 30- to 45-day follow-up and the 1-year surveys of new owners, they should be distributed and analyzed as follows:

- Establish a tickler file by week or month that extends over a 2-year period. At closing, insert into this file for each new owner two survey packages—each containing a survey questionnaire and cover letter from you or your market research firm (if applicable), plus a stamped return envelope addressed to either you or your market research firm (1-year survey).
- Make a clerical person on your staff responsible for mailing the envelopes from the tickler file each week or month throughout the year.
- Collect and submit responses from the 30- to 45-day survey in bulk to the market research firm semi-annually or annually (annually for most small-volume builders with 50 or fewer sales) or maintain an internal tabulation and analysis with spreadsheet software on your computer. Similarly collect, tabulate, and analyze responses from the 1-year survey annually.
- Computer tabulation and analysis of completed questionnaires normally requires a month, and you should schedule them prior to completing your annual marketing plan and budget—for example, questionnaire tabulation and analysis in November for marketing plan and budget preparation in December of each year.

Completing the analysis of both surveys simultaneously allows you to compare responses on similar types of questions. In addition, both types of information provide valuable input to your annual marketing plan and budget process.

New owner surveys of your competitor's purchasers as well as your own purchasers provide valuable comparisons. The same questionnaires can be used, but the response rate will be higher if the sponsor is a market research firm rather than a builder.

Proxy Opinion Surveys

In order to reduce costs and time, proxy opinion surveys collect consumer opinions through telephone or personal interviews with new home sales persons who specialize in a particular type of consumer.

In one such survey, the best-selling active adult communities in a Sunbelt market were identified and telephone interviews conducted with sales persons in each community about consumer origins and their choices of models, features, and options. Another proxy opinion survey was conducted by telephone of salespersons for small-lot communities near a proposed small-lot subdivision acquisition to ascertain purchaser geodemographics as well as choices of models, features, and options.

For both of these surveys, time and cost was 40 to 50 percent lower than for a consumer opinion survey, and the decision-makers for the builder-developer received the responses 3 weeks from inception of the survey.

Focus Groups

Qualitative market research techniques have evolved over the past three decades primarily through the use of focus group interviewing. This technique involves asking questions of a selected group of 8 to 12 people rather than the traditional individual questionnaire used in quantitative surveys. Sessions usually last 2 hours. Group questioning stimulates interactive discussion by members of the group and produces collective answers subject to interpretation. These answers often reveal emotional motivations not available from statistical response data.

Because focus group results are subject to the interviewer's biases, having experienced professionals conduct this type of research is essential. Specially designed discussion rooms with observer space behind one-way glass and videotaping facilities are available in many markets through companies that do focus group research. Figure 1.11 illustrates a focus group session in a special purpose discussion room.

The professional focus group leader coordinates the discussion to elicit a full range of opinions from participants on key issues defined in advance by the focus group leader and builder-developer. You should learn the preferences of the participants, their reactions to particular home styles and features, and reactions to community amenities as well as location strengths and weaknesses. Experts in this field usually recommend a minimum of two or three such groups to thoroughly explore a set of design and marketing issues.

Builder-Developer Application

Many builders appear to believe that focus groups and consumer surveys are too expensive for their use. However, costs are declining and the results are valuable. You also can take advantage of wider market surveys by others such as the national consumer preference surveys conducted by the National Association of Home

FIGURE 1.11 Focus Group Session

Builders, industry magazine surveys, and local surveys sponsored by government and financial institutions.

Diane Morrison, director of marketing for Morrison Homes in Austin, Texas, reports a four-step process to determine cost-effective marketing for her company. The process begins by clarifiying target consumers, using one of the above-described survey techniques or internal team brainstorming. Subsequent steps are based upon this thorough understanding of target consumers: determine visitor projections for defined products, select the best media to reach those consumers, and create an appealing message targeted to these consumers.

Understanding the target consumer requires qualitative information on personalities, lifestyles, and preferences as well as quantitative data on age, income, household size, and current location. If a development is large-scale and requires several years for buildout, then you must project current consumer characteristics to ascertain probable market shifts.

You can use each of the consumer survey techniques to learn valuable information about your own purchasers, your prospective purchasers, and even your competition's purchasers. You should consult market research specialists to determine the most efficient applications for your proposed developments.

Competition

The competition includes new homes offered for sale in the market area of your proposed site that might appeal to the same consumers you intend to target. Often comparing information on your competition with your information on consumer preferences will reveal comparative advantages you can exploit to gain a favorable position over your competition. Research on the competition should reveal dwelling price, size, value (price per square foot of heated and cooled area), and standard features. With this information you can design product offerings that improve upon the competition. Community and local area amenities (including schools, recreation, and shopping) also may vary among competition locations. Annual or monthly sales rates identify the competitive products receiving the best consumer response as a guide to projecting sales absorption for your proposed products. This profile provides the context in which you must compete.

Product Supply

The supply of new homes in a specific marketplace varies continually by both number and type, it depends on the separate decisions of the home builders active in the area. Usually no central depository exists where information on new homes is kept current. Permit data from the local government building department usually provide the best indicator of new homes activity. However, not all permits result in completed dwellings, and those that do include model homes and speculative dwellings not sold to consumers in any given time period. Recorded real estate transactions include lots as well as both resale homes and new homes without differentiation, and dwellings often are constructed by contract after a lot transaction is recorded. Many cities contain real estate data services that monitor new home sales either by recorded sales transactions in identified new homes subdivisions or by regular surveys of the sales staffs in these subdivisions. These data services records provide useful data, but they are not comprehensive in terms of new home sales outside the identified subdivisions.

Thus, for a particular location, builders usually must obtain data on the supply of competitive houses by monitoring identified competitive developments to determine the five key characteristics of new homes offerings: price, size, value, features, amenities, and sales rates. Figure 1.12 illustrates the distribution of competitive product offerings by price, dwelling size, and value ratio in a particular market. Figure 1.13 illustrates the frequency of dwelling features and community amenities in this same market. Figure 1.14 lists sales absorption by competitive property. It indicates both overall sales absorption since initiation of sales as well as current year sales absorption.

Competitive Product Records

A relatively simple format for recording data on competitive (or comparable) developments or individual homes appears in Figure 1.15. This form can be completed successfully by anyone familiar with the housing business. With a little experience, you or a staff member can visit eight to ten developments and record their products in a single day.

Figure 1.16 illustrates one type of summary form used to record the information collected through field research. While this form provides columns for a full range of housing types, you may want to revise the top of the form for a single dwelling type that is your primary competition.

Figure 1.17 is an example of summarized field data collected by professional analysts for a specific market of dwellings. The distance in miles from the subject property is noted, along with information on total dwellings, sales rates, price, size, calculated value ratio, home and community amenities, and association fees. Assuming consumer demand is sufficient to proceed with an additional product offering in this market, the information on this page can position the new product advantageously over the competition.

Results of this research are summarized in the graphs presented in Figures 1.12, 1.13, and 1.14 for better understanding of the competitive marketplace. You can compare your new product offerings with these graphic distributions to assess your position with regard to competitive price, size, value, benefits and features, and amenities.

You can obtain more accurate price information by identifying actual sales transactions while examining county records. However, such an examination may prove costly unless a specific information service is available in your market area at modest cost.

Sales Absorption

Sales absorption, or rate of sales, depends upon many factors, including uncertain national and local economic conditions, product acceptance, and marketing effectiveness. To project sales absorption for financial feasibility and planning purposes, the safest method bases future sales absorption on experience, either your own experience or that of competitive builders selling comparable homes.

FIGURE 1.12 Price, Size, and Value Distribution

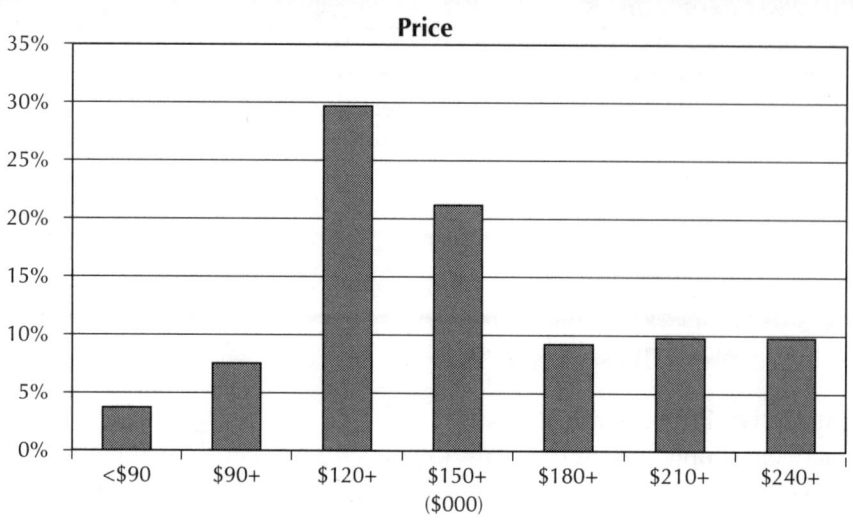

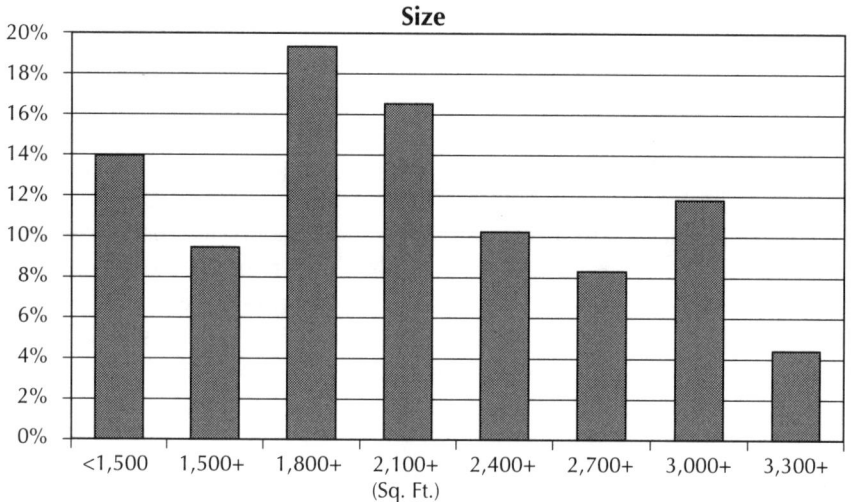

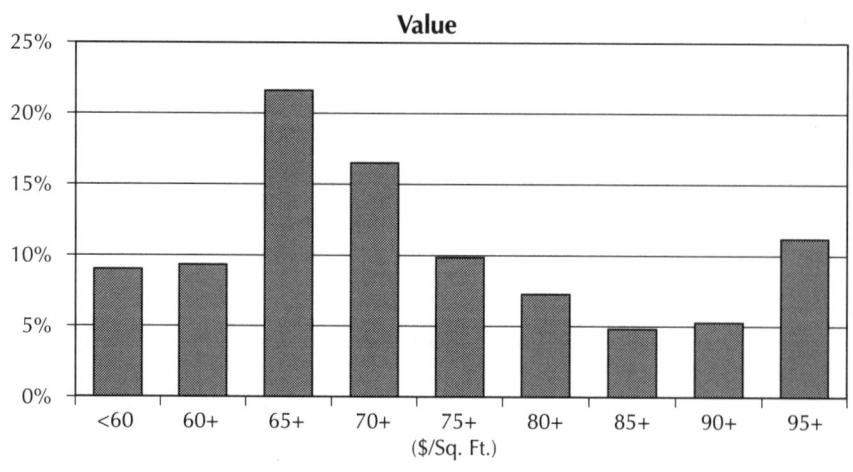

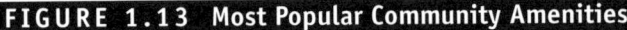

FIGURE 1.13 Most Popular Community Amenities

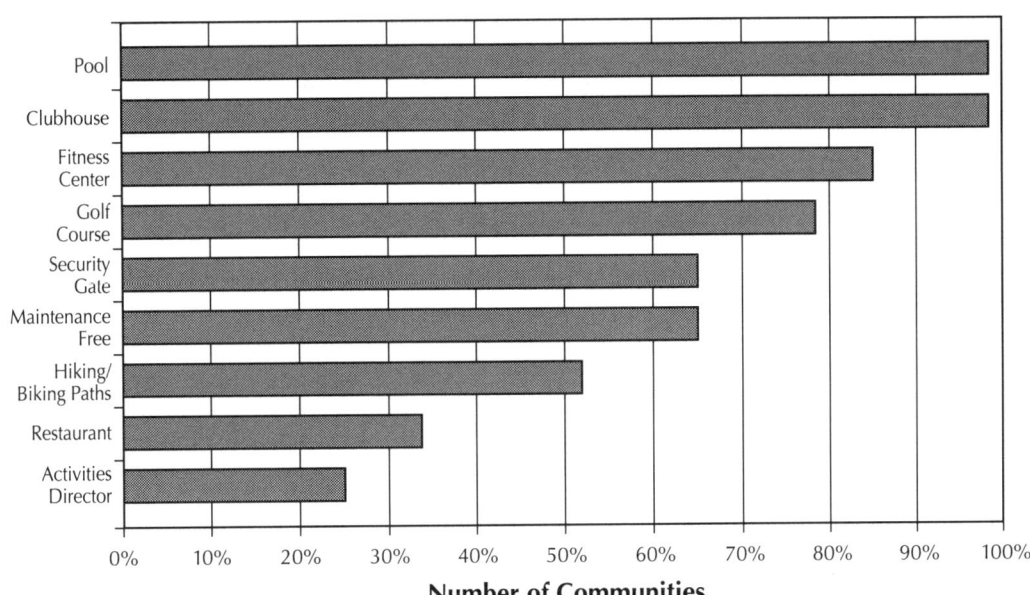

Number of Communities

FIGURE 1.14 Sales Absorption by Competitive Property

Map Code	Development	Builders	Price Range ($000) Min - Max	LOTS/DWELLINGS Width	Lot Size (sf)	Total	Available	Sold	Total Months Selling	Average Monthly Absorp.	On-Site Amenities Pool	Gated	Golf Front
1	Westbury Lakes @ Rosedale	Rosedale Construction	152 - 179	47'	5,170	40	33	7	11	0.6	No	Yes	No
2	Summerfield Forest @ Lakewood	Bovis Homes	121 - 127	50'	5,750	40	5	35	26	1.3	Yes	No	No
3	Somerset @ Turtle Rock	Lee Wetherington	184 - 199	50'	6,000	66	12	54	22	2.5	No	No	No
4	Edgewater Cove @ Lakewood	Pulte Master Builders	153 - 186	52'	5,720	100	35	65	23	2.8	Yes	Yes	No
5	Savannah @ Turtle Rock	Donovan Homes	190 - 210	52'	5,720	82	25	57	36	1.6	No	Yes	No
6	The Arbors @ Pelican Pointe	Ryland Homes	144 - 180	52'	6,240	178	162	16	6	2.7	No	Yes	Yes
7	Muirfield @ Lakewood Ranch	Neal Communities	148 - 190	52'	6,500	64	29	35	18	1.9	Yes	Yes	Yes
8	Notting Hill @ University Park	Neal Communities	171 - 192	52'	7,280	52	18	34	24	1.4	Yes	Yes	No
8	The Greens @ Pelican Pointe	Rodgers/Rutenberg	140 - 170	55'	6,050	99	28	71	36	2.0	No	Yes	Yes
10	The Hamptons on Palmer Ranch	Lennar Homes	172 - 187	57'	6,840	141	133	8	8	1.0	No	Yes	No
1	Clubview Crossing @ Rosedale	Rosedale Const.	198 - 230	57'	6,270	46	18	28	18	1.6	No	Yes	Yes
11	Southwood @ River Club	Several	149 - 179	60'	6,600	113	12	101	48	2.1	No	No	Yes
12	Falcon Trace @ Calusa Lakes	Nisley Homes	160 - 162	60'	6,600	38	19	19	24	0.8	No	Yes	Yes
13	Bermuda Club @ Plantation G&CC	Whitehall Homes	175 - 205	60'	7,200	30	19	21	15	1.4	No	Yes	Yes
14	The Greens @ El Conquistador	Neal Communities	166 - 245	60'	9,000	43	8	35	20	1.8	No	No	No
8	Wentworth @ University Park	Neal Communities	205 - 261	62'	8,680	46	3	43	18	2.4	No	Yes	No
6	Fairway Oaks @ Pelican Pointe	Rutenberg	188 - 221	70'	7,700	99	16	83	40	2.1	No	Yes	No
12	Eagles Nest @ Calusa Lakes	Nisley Homes	187 - 299	94'	12,690	39	13	26	24	1.1	No	Yes	Yes
	TOTALS					1,316	588	738			22%	78%	44%
	AVERAGES		167 - 202		7,001	73	33	41	23	1.7			

Note The Palisades @ Palmer Ranch is omitted due to the short period of time they have been open. No sales were indicated. Pool on site.
    Ascot @ University Park is excluded as well for the above reason; two contracts pending. No pool on site.

FIGURE 1.15 Competitive Evaluation

Shopper _____ Date _____

Development Name _____ Developer _____

Address _____

Type of Development
☐ single family detached, large lot"
☐ small lot/zero lot line detached
☐ attached
☐ multi-level ___ number of stories
☐ resort

Location Features (e.g. riverfront, heavily wooded, etc.) _____

_____

Phase # _____ # Dwellings _____ # Starts _____ # Sales _____

Product or Model
    #BR/BA   Base Price   Sq. Ft.   Price/Sq. Ft.

1_____ _____ _____ _____

2 _____ _____ _____ _____

3 _____ _____ _____ _____

Price Range—(low to high) $ _____ to $ _____

Site Amenities (e.g. pool, tennis, etc.) _____

Car Parking
☐ Uncovered   ☐ Single Garage   ☐ Structure Parking
☐ Carport   ☐ Double Garage

Dwelling Features (special standard features) _____

Dwelling Features (special optional features available) _____

The comparative experience method of projecting sales absorption relies upon reasonably reliable information about sales absorption of competitive product offerings. (Generally this method avoids offerings on the market less than 6 months because initial in-house or investor sales tend to skew the sales records.) Assuming that you market your planned new offerings effectively, you can reasonably assume that (a) your sales absorption will exceed the average of all competitive products, but (b) it will not exceed the best-selling competitive products. If the range between the average and the best-selling competitive offering is substantial (for example, 100 percent), then a realistic judgement call is required—how will acceptance of your new home offering compare with that of the top competition? You must apply this test to set realistic sales absorption rates.

Regardless of the final decision on sales absorption, you must vary absorption by development stage as well as by season of the year. Except in unusual cases in which demand far exceeds supply, a new product (especially in a new community) will not achieve immediate market acceptance. Sales absorption will increase over time as the community matures and as happy owners tell their friends and create referrals. Present-day Americans generally are not pioneers or risk-takers when it comes to buying homes. They are more likely to purchase where others have purchased before them.

FIGURE 1.16 Product Definition Form

| Product Definition | Dwelling Type | | | | | |
| | Detached | | Attached | | Multi Story | |
	Full	Patio	Townhouse	TH/Flat	Walk-Up	Elevator
Dwelling Size Bedrooms Bathroom H/C Square Feet						
Dwelling Features Kitchen microwave ice maker disposal compactor washer/dryer						
Living fireplace wet bar entertainment ctr built-ins volume ceilings special flooring						
Exterior garage (,2) patio/balcony hot tubs special landscape						
Development Amenities Security Gate Swimming Pool(s) Hot Tub(s) Tennis Courts Racquetball Courts Exercise Room Jogging Trail Club House Lakes/Beach Boat Docks						

FIGURE 1.17   Competitive/Comparable Development Form

Development _____

Address _____

Date _____

By: _____
_____ (name)

Distance From Subject Property: _____

Type of Development: _____

Price Range: _____

Location Feature: _____

Date Sales Started: _____

Monthly Sales Rate: _____

Avg. Monthly Traffic: _____

Dwellings Under Construction: _____

Building Height: _____

No. of Buildings: _____

Dwelling Type	BR/BA	No. of Dwellings			Selling Price	Dwlg Size Sq. Ft. H/C Area	Price Per Sq. Ft. H/C Area	Monthly Maintenance Fee
		Planned	Completed	Sold				
____	____	____	____	____	____	____	____	____
____	____	____	____	____	____	____	____	____
____	____	____	____	____	____	____	____	____
____	____	____	____	____	____	____	____	____
____	____	____	____	____	____	____	____	____
____	____	____	____	____	____	____	____	____
____	____	____	____	____	____	____	____	____
____	____	____	____	____	____	____	____	____
TOTAL		____	____	____				

Site Amenities: _____

Car Parking: _____

Purchaser Characteristics: _____

Dwelling Features: _____

Price Premiums: _____

Comments: _____

Sales absorption also varies by season of the year in most parts of the country. You can assess the extent of this seasonal variation in a particular marketplace by examining monthly sales on the multiple listing service (MLS) of the local board of Realtors® over a multiyear period.

Define the Right Product

The information on consumer demand and competitive products provides a basis for defining the best product(s) for profitability at this location. This process begins with a concept of the most competitive product(s) including dwellings and community amenities. You need to price proposed dwellings according to competitive prices and lot location premiums. You can achieve the highest revenues by (a) adjusting the mix of offerings to projected sales rates for each product type and (b) ensuring community amenities suitable for your target consumers. The dwelling design process must ensure that final product offerings include consumer preferences.

The Product Definition Process

Figure 1.18 summarizes the full product definition process for a new residential community or neighborhood based upon the results of your marketing feasibility study. Concept formation for the site and buildings is derived from the three key feasibility components:

- consumer demand
- competitive product supply

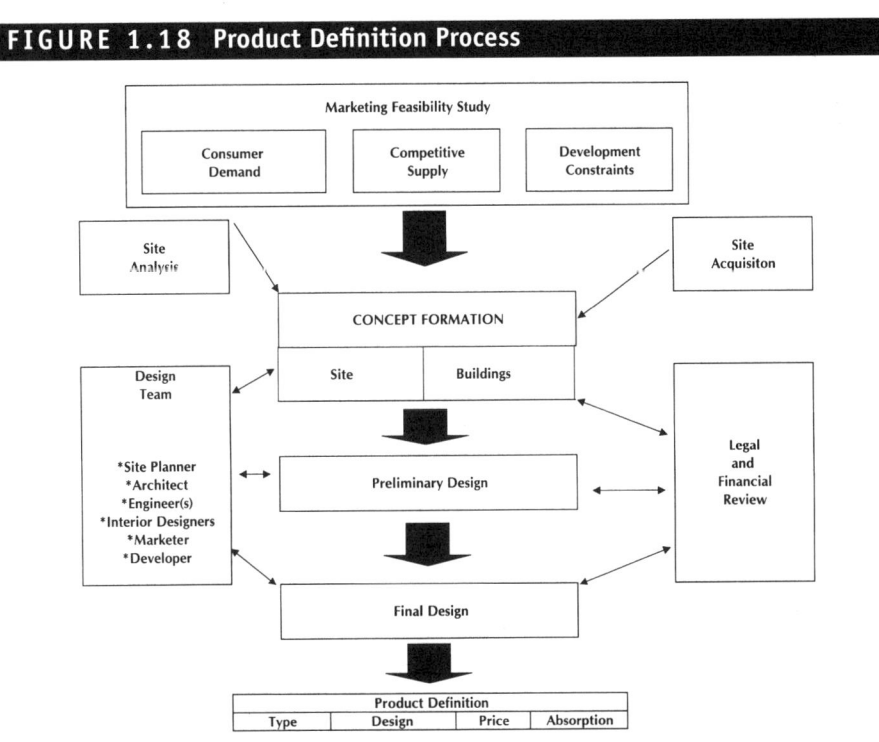

FIGURE 1.18 Product Definition Process

■ development constraints

The concept is refined by analyzing a specific acquired site and through a review by the design team and legal and financial specialists. This interactive decision process continues through preliminary and final design stages, with a critical appraisal of increasing levels of detail by each team member. The result is an optimum product for a specific market and time period, with the final sales product defined in terms of dwelling type, design, price, and rate of sales absorption. The following discussion of product positioning and community and home selection will help you define a new product. While your professional judgment remains paramount, systematically organizing the decision process will improve the odds of success.

Positioning New Homes

Most people practice positioning every day when they engage in conversation with others, take a seat at a conference or dinner table, or play competitive sports. Positioning helps an individual achieve a location or condition of advantage.

Positioning is a term frequently employed by advertising agencies to denote the best way to present a particular product with respect to estimated consumer needs and preferences. The objective is to communicate the appeal of the product in a more advantageous manner than competitive products. However, regardless of the widely acclaimed skills of the American advertising industry, successful positioning must begin with product design. While a badly designed product might generate consumer acceptance through clever advertising, it will place a poor second in competition with a product that is both well designed and well marketed.

Accurate Positioning. Beginning with initial property acquisition, accurate positioning of new homes extends through product design, marketing, selling, and customer service activities. The best position for a new home and or new home community is the one that promises the highest competitive advantage in a specific marketplace.

Know the Prospect. Positioning is also based upon knowledge of prospective buyers. It not only defines and designs products for targeted consumers, but it also communicates to potential consumers the features designed just for them. Targeted consumers thus become aware of the care and attention given to their needs and preferences and are impressed, both rationally and emotionally, because competitive products frequently lack this care. Effective positioning results in more and faster sales.

Positioning Costs. The best news is that positioning is not necessarily more expensive than not positioning. It is accomplished through perceptive control and coordination, and it often results in more disciplined, cost-effective marketing approaches. Increasing numbers of builders are discovering that positioning is essential to successfully selling new homes.

Choose the Right Community

When planning or selecting a community, you translate marketing feasibility findings into specific community guidelines, including the amenities selected for optimum positioning. You should exercise as much or more care in planning or selecting a community than in designing a new home, for the fact is well established that consumers choose a neighborhood prior to selecting a home. The key factors in choosing the right community are—

- location
- approach image
- site plan
- amenities
- lot price

Location. Location continues to be the leading influence guiding home purchases. Therefore the best location for a home or community is that part of the market area considered most desirable by the targeted consumers. For example, housing for seniors often proves attractive when it is located within walking distance of shopping, and family-oriented, first move-up homes often sell rapidly within walking distance of an elementary school.

Approach Image. To some extent, you can manipulate a new community's approach image by improving the property perimeter and entrance. However, improvements beyond the subject property are unlikely. A first-time purchaser on a limited budget may well disregard unsightly conditions on the approach road to a particularly well-priced development, but more affluent third and fourth move-up purchasers are usually sensitive to the image of their proposed new community and its environs.

Site Plan. The site plan can have a substantial impact on prospective buyers. The haphazard, seemingly random road patterns of the 1950s are as unsatisfactory to today's single-family home buyers as the rigid grid plans of the pre-World War II era. (Chapter 2 discusses neotraditional site plans.) Most people prefer an address that is relatively easy to locate but, at the same time, is distinctive with respect to neighborhood location and not just another number on a straight line of homes. Everyone wants something special. Therefore you need to carefully critique the best site plans with respect to the attractiveness of every lot.

Traditionally, planners and developers focused on physical design as a means of fostering community. But now successful community developers must consider creating opportunities for social activities as a way to draw residents together. Increasing numbers of discriminating consumers will focus on the civic infrastructure for public health, education, telecommunications, community organizations, and civic leadership as being more important than the physical infrastructure of streets, utilities, parks, schools, and other public facilities. As a visionary builder, you must understand this shift in consumer preferences and select your sites accordingly.

Amenities. Community amenities include both the natural characteristics of the property and man-made improvements. A recent focus group of first-time purchasers revealed trees are the single most sought-after community characteristic, including man-made improvements. Clearly, preserving trees should be a primary concern of every builder and developer. Lakes, hills, and other natural characteristics also add value to a new community.

The appeal of man-made amenities varies tremendously among consumer groups. Empty nesters are attracted by 24-hour security, while first-time purchasers with children consider it an unnecessary expense. They prefer to invest their limited funds in additional living space. Many budget-conscious consumers feel the same way about swimming pools, tennis courts, and other recreational amenities. However, professional couples often are attracted by such amenities.

Lot Price. Inexperienced builders often assume the unfortunate attitude that negotiations for lots should focus on price. Certainly, lot price is important, and its percentage of the final product price should be within the acceptable range for the local market. However, you must remember that lot price is only one of several key variables in successful product definition. The four factors described above may prove much more important to your ultimate sales rate and profitability than lot price.

Choose the Right Homes

Only a small proportion of communities achieve a happy marriage of land and buildings. These homes may not all win national design awards, but they do produce rapid sales and happy owners. Street image, exterior design, efficient floor plans, and special features all must blend to match the tastes of targeted consumers. You must consider special development issues of the future in addressing consumer preference, including rising costs of materials, use of new materials (for example, synthetics), and the increasing influences of environmental interests in the production of raw materials as well as in neighborhood design.

Details of dwelling types are addressed in Chapter 2. The key issue addressed here is one of matching each dwelling type to specific consumer types. An effective means of determining product mix for either a community or small number of homes is the consumer-product profile. In this profile, consumer demand is distributed among those selected housing types the builder prefers to build and/or those permitted by local ordinance.

New home consumers are best classified according to household types that need and/or prefer various types of homes and communities. Although housing preferences may vary within each consumer group, the majority of each group will prefer specific types, sizes, and prices of dwellings in each marketplace.

While definitions abound for consumer groups, and clever new words and phrases emerge continually, the classifications discussed in the following paragraphs have effectively matched consumer groups to housing types:

Singles. The number of single households is increasing throughout the country as younger people postpone marriage and the high rate of divorce continues. Singles come in all age groups, though the higher proportions are younger singles under age 30 and older singles (primarily females) over age 75. Many singles prefer one-bedroom dwellings. Others will opt for two-bedroom homes with equal or approximately equal bedrooms. Many moderate-income singles choose a second bedroom or den for conversion to an office or work space at home.

Tandems. Two nonconjugal persons sharing a dwelling, tandems purchase homes either under single ownership plus lease agreement or through dual ownership. They require at least two bedroom suites with full bathrooms and large closets. Such living arrangements are becoming more common, and because of dual incomes, often constitute a significant consumer group for higher priced, low-maintenance homes. Preference for the subject property should be similar to singles.

Single Parents. Single parents are separated, divorced, widowed, or never-married persons who tend to be under 50 with one or more children living with them. They primarily rent or purchase low-priced two- and three-bedroom homes.

Couples. The U.S. Census data define this category as married. Changing lifestyles suggest redefining this group as conjugating couples regardless of marital status or sexual preference. These couples are further defined below.

Professional Couples. Defined as two conjugating persons who are both employed as income earners, professional couples can afford more expensive accommodations than single-income households. These couples can be of any age (although those over 45 tend to exhibit characteristics similar to empty nesters and are often termed never nesters). They generally opt for two- and three-bedroom homes, though many prefer and can afford larger homes.

Traditional Couples. Childless married couples with one spouse employed, traditional couples span all age groups but tend toward the low price ranges because of the single income. They are often couples planning to have children; therefore, their interests center on three- and four-bedroom homes.

Empty Nesters. Defined as married couples with one or both spouses employed and grown children who no longer live with them, these consumers require larger than average two-bedroom (or more) homes to accommodate their furnishings and family visitors. Empty nesters also require substantial storage space.

Seniors. These people are generally retired or semiretired couples and singles who prefer smaller and lower-maintenance residences than younger persons. Although retirees need only one- or two-bedrooms, space for their lifelong possessions is an important factor in retiree housing.

Couples with Children. These couples include both one- and two-income earners who require at least two bedrooms and generally are younger than 45 years of age. They usually prefer detached homes, but many (particularly young families and reconstituted families of limited income) choose small lot or attached homes. In more urban markets, they may chose multifamily rental or ownership (condominium) dwellings.

Predicting consumer demand from each of the above-described groups for a particular home or community requires logical reasoning rather than mathematical logic. You must analyze the demand and supply data and use creative judgement in estimating consumer demand by product type.

Figure 1.19 provides an example of a typical consumer-product profile that estimates demand for each appropriate consumer type and distributes that demand according to housing types selected for this property. Projected zoning and subdivision approvals provide an estimate of the total number of homes anticipated on the property. This information allows translation of demand percentages into home sales for each consumer group and type of home. To calculate price, compare competitive offerings (as described in the earlier description of competitive product supply). At this stage, prior to product design, the builder establishes a price range for each dwelling type to estimate a range of potential revenues. Based on the projected revenue, the builder eventually develops an overall assessment of financial feasibility.

Projecting Annual Revenues

You can anticipate that sales will increase as the community gains publicity in your marketplace and concurrently becomes increasingly settled with new residents; sales will decline as choices become limited in the final stage of selling. Normally you can increase prices in concert with increasing absorption. Annual revenues are calculated from annual sales multiplied by dwelling prices plus price increases. Revenues minus development costs provide annual cash flow and subsequent financial feasibility for the entire development.

Figure 1.20 provides an example of a projection of annual revenues using projected annual sales absorption figures factored by the average sales price (exclusive of options) of each new home offering. As noted previously, consumers are more likely to purchase after many homes are occupied, so absorption tends to increase with occupancy and annual revenues increase accordingly.

This increase in consumer interest as the difficult pioneer phase changes into the maturing community or neighborhood stage with greater numbers of rooftops complete is accompanied by increasing product value. That is, your offerings become worth more money in the eyes of the consumer as the community or neighborhood matures. This property appreciation is reflected in the table in

FIGURE 1.19 Consumer/Product Profile

Consumers	Sales Demand	2 Bdrm	2 Master Bdrm	2 Bdrm & Den	3 Bdrm	Pent-house	Total Sales
Tandem Singles	10%	—	10%	—	—	—	25
Young Professionals	15%	10	—	5	—	—	37
Empty Nesters	55%	15	5	25	7	3	37
Near Empty Nesters	20%	—	—	—	17	3	50
Total Percent	100	25	15	30	24	6	—
Total Dwellings	62	38	75	60	15	250	
Low Price	$0	190	225	245	285	390	—
Total Revenue	$0	11,780	8550	18.375	17,100	5,850	61,655
High Price	$(000)	215	240	275	315	450	—
Total Revenue	$(000)	13330	9120	20625	18900	6750	68725

Mean Revenue Potential: $65.2 million
Mean Revenue Potential Per Building: $16.3 million

FIGURE 1.20 Housing Absorption Schedule

	YEARS:	-0.5	1	2	3	3.5	TOTAL	
Small Lot Dwellings								
A	2500 sf	1	3	5	5	3	17	
B	2350 sf	2	8	8	8	5	31	
C	2200 sf	1	8	8	8	4	29	
D	2050 sf	0	3	6	6	3	18	
	SUB TOTAL	4	22	27	27	15	95	
Patio Lot Dwellings								
X	2100 sf	1	6	8	8	3	26	
Y	1950 sf	1	8	8	8	6	31	
Z	1800 sf	0	6	8	8	3	25	
	SUB TOTAL	2	20	24	24	12	82	
TOTAL		6	42	51	51	27	177	
	PERCENT	0.03	0.24	0.29	0.29	0.15	1.00	
BASE PRICE	$000							LOTS
A	233	233	698	1,163	1,163	698	3,953	870
B	223	445	1,780	1,780	1,780	1,113	6,898	1,517
C	213	213	1,700	1,700	1,700	850	6,163	1,356
D	203	-	608	1,215	1,215	608	3,645	802
X	197	197	1,179	1,572	1,572	590	5,109	971
Y	187	187	1,492	1,492	1,492	1,119	5,782	1,098
Z	176	-	1,053	1,404	1,404	527	4,388	834
PREMIUMS+	9.9	59	416	505	505	267	1,752	1,752
TOTAL		1,332	8,925	10,830	10,830	5,770	37,468	9,089
PERCENT		4	24	29	29	15	100	
PRICE INCREASE		1.00	1.00	1.02	1.04	1.04		
REVISED TOTAL		1,332	8,925	11,047	11,264	6,001	38,568	9,356
AVG PRICE/DWLG							218	53

Note: All base lot revenues are in 1998 dollar values (i.e. no inflation factor).

Source: Parker Associates, April 1998.

Figure 1.20 by an annual price escalation exclusive of any addition for inflation. The scale of this escalation depends upon the intensity of consumer demand in your market, but generally is adjusted upwards or downwards from 2 percent with respect to achievement of sales projections.

Thus, in projecting annual revenues you are well advised to relate them directly to realistic sales projections with appropriate lag time for construction and closing. Although the addition of price escalation relative to development maturity is realistic, you may prefer to exclude it to ensure a more conservative annual revenues projection. The relationship of sales absorption and revenues projection to marketing expenditures is presented in Chapter 3.

2

Select the Best Site, Lots, and Dwelling Types

The site selection process is most builders' biggest business decision. The following discussion of selection follows the builder's normal sequence: site selection, dwelling types, and due diligence. This section also addresses using computer systems to help locate available sites, the emerging potential of redevelopment sites, and the best means of expanding to new markets.

Site Selection

Site selection means choosing from the lots available in the marketplace at a particular time rather than deliberately searching for sites defined by market analysis. Alternatively it may include undertaking your own land development, or it may be restricted to acquiring lots in a land developer's existing or planned development. In either case, you should consider each of the following 12 criteria prior to conducting the detailed market research described later under Due Diligence.

Location. Location continues to be the leading influence guiding home purchases. Therefore, the best location for building a new home or community is that part of the market area considered most desirable by the targeted consumer. For example, housing for older seniors often proves attractive when located within walking distance of shopping and health care, and family-oriented first move-up homes often sell well when located within walking distance of an elementary school. The quality of area schools is a critical factor for family households; area recreation facilities and convenience goods shopping centers are important to all consumers. Although specific consumer research may be required to support location selection, most builders are sufficiently familiar with their marketplace to evaluate overall location parameters. As stated by Denver land planner and author David Jensen, "today's homebuyers do not just purchase a house on a lot. They purchase homes in neighborhoods and the emotions which they evoke—the 'look and live' of new communities." For sites located in master planned communities, Jensen states that new home buyers are influenced by the periphery of the property along the community boundary, the entry to the community, the major identity elements of the community such as a lake, a community center and/or a park, the drive through the community to its neighborhoods, and the local street character. You must consider these elements as you evaluate the location of a proposed building site.

Financial Terms. For most builders, even those with extensive funding capability, attractive financial terms for site acquisition are second only to location in the decision process. Overall price may not prove to be as important as (a) the required cash deposit and payment schedule or (b) a substantial discount from fair market value for an all-cash purchase. The cash discount may be the deciding factor for builders with investment capital. You must evaluate each prospective site acquisition on the basis of your financial situation, but you need to make this assessment early in the selection process to avoid wasting time on sites that are not financially feasible.

Development Cost. For undeveloped land acquisition, or for developed lots on land with steep grades or unusual soil conditions, you should evaluate assumed development costs in concert with financial terms. They constitute an addition to the total purchase price or a supplement to a payment schedule.

Lot Size. If the proposed site is already platted, you must evaluate lot size in terms of known demand by targeted consumers. You do not need to take the risk of being a pioneer on an untested lot size without the benefit of strong consumer research to support the lot size. In the absence of such research, select sites with lot sizes that are already popular in your marketplace.

Site Plan. The increasing influence of neotraditional site planners—the *new urbanists*—during the 1990s evoked greater sensitivity to site planning by new home purchasers as well as builders. The lot-size decision is interwoven with the site-plan decision in what often appears to be a largely emotional process that is strongly influenced by marketing effectiveness for particular sites. Kentlands in metropolitan Washington and Celebration in metropolitan Orlando have capitalized on apparent consumer demand for the relatively small lots and minimum private open space of neotraditional site plans. However, the extent of this demand nationwide, particularly in smaller marketplaces, is unproven. Until more solid evidence of consumer demand is available, neotraditional site plans must be considered an unmeasurable risk for most builders.

According to community developer John Martin writing in *Urban Land* ("Building Community," March 1996), "neotraditionalism is simply one of many valuable approaches to consider . . . in our nation's increasingly diverse and seg-mented housing markets." Because most such planned communities are still works in progress, they cannot be adequately evaluated. You can expect further development experiments to emerge in future years. Each neotraditional com-munity requires objective evaluation research before it can become a sound devel-opment investment for most builders.

Timing Development. Undeveloped land or finished lots that must be held for long periods rarely achieve financial success. Therefore you should select sites that are in the path of future development. You need lot locations for homes that can be sold in the near future to avoid uncertain regional and local economic changes because those changes can cause demand for a particular product or location to evaporate quickly.

Developer Responsibilities. When purchasing finished lots, you should define the precise responsibilities of the lot developer in the purchase agreement. Infrastructure, landscaping, and amenities illustrated on a master plan may be only illustrative if not clearly defined in terms of both scale and timing in your agreement. Do not be misled by pretty pictures.

Community Amenities. Parks, play fields, swimming pools, tennis courts, club-houses, golf courses, and other amenities proposed in a planned community may be critical factors for a purchaser prior to deciding on one of your new homes. If the developer does not deliver them as promised, your sales will not materialize as projected and your credibility as a builder will be damaged. Site selection within a master planned community proposing such amenities must be based upon a pre-cise written agreement defining their scale and construction schedule.

Environmental Factors. Air quality, ground quality, flooding potential, noise pollution, and traffic congestion all constitute environmental factors that may not require government approval control over a new development but may seriously affect its appeal to future homeowners. Examine the potential affect of each of these and related environmental factors prior to reaching a decision on site selection.

Nearby Competition. You should evaluate the characteristics, success, and longevity of competitive offerings near a proposed site for potential impact on your proposed offerings. A rapidly selling development in a higher price range than your offerings should constitute a positive impact on your sales whereas a slow-selling lower-priced development near your site could have a negative impact on your sales. A nearby development priced similarly to your proposed offerings could be advantageous if you believe you can provide a clear comparative advan-tage over these offerings, particularly if this nearby development is nearing sellout.

Local Political Climate. Local governments vary widely in their support for new residential development. Small towns and old suburbs that have not experi-enced recent new development often prefer to oppose it to maintain their cur-rent lifestyle (often the amenity that attracts new home builders and purchasers). Political leaders in such locations may believe their responsibility is to enforce restrictive zoning and building codes to increase both development and building costs. On the other hand, you may find local politicians who welcome growth opportunities and thereby ensure faster development approvals and lower costs. You need to evaluate the local political climate prior to considering product pricing in a proposed new location.

Imagination and Creativity. Planner David Jensen believes that imagination is possibly the most important, and most often overlooked, attribute in selecting new development sites: "Many sites appear to have development constraints such as size, limited access, wetlands, numerous drainage ways, steep topography, protected wildlife habitat, etc. . . . a skilled land planner can turn these constraints into natural amenities which ultimately result in lot premiums and substantially increased home sales.' Jensen adds that only "innovative and creative land planning can capture the value inherent in many sites . . . many projects can be imagined, it most often requires creative solutions to implement them."

Each of the criteria listed above apply to builders selecting a few lots in a community planned by a developer as well as those builders prepared to develop lots from unimproved land. If you purchase lots in an existing or planned community, the value of that community impacts your potential home purchaser. If you are planning a new community, you have the opportunity to ensure your community's value from its inception by observing these 12 criteria of site selection.

If you begin with defined selection criteria and a general location area, but no specific sites, you may want to enlist the aid of computer programs designed to identify potential sites for you. The Geographic Information System (GIS), a computer software program for site selection, is offered by some planning and engineering firms as one of their services. It can identify land parcels in a geographic area by a variety of parameters including size, zoning, ownership, peripheral services, and physical characteristics. You can identify priority sites without leaving the office.

When evaluating new market areas for your products, utilize the principles of market research described in Chapter 1 of this book, especially identifiying consumers and their preferences. Once objective analysis reveals potential areas for your products, GIS described above can identify possible sites for acquisition. Visual inspection can be deferred until electronic data processing equips you with basic information on available sites.

A final note on site selection is the recommendation to include urban redevelopment locations in your continuing search for new sites. As suburban sites become increasingly expensive to purchase and develop and as traffic congestion makes commuting more traumatic, increasing numbers of builders will examine the potential of developing urban housing on redevelopment sites. Do not overlook this possibility in your future site selection actions. Again GIS can provide a means for efficient exploration.

Dwelling Types

In selecting dwelling designs to be offered at a particular site, you should be guided by research on consumer preferences and competitive trends to discern potential market niches (unfulfilled consumer demand). For example, an Atlanta builder learned that prospective purchasers of small dwellings were concerned about separating activities in small homes with single living areas. In response, the architect created an enlarged bedroom hall with nooks for a computer desk, toy storage, or television for all children in the family. You should examine the selected dwelling types for pricing suitability, absorption potential, and profit potential prior to a final decision. You also need to address the issues discussed in the following paragraphs as part of this decision process on dwelling types.

Work with the Architect

The essence of successful builder home design is an efficient working relationship between the builder and the architect or residential designer. For best results you must provide the architect with design guidelines for the dwelling or dwellings you require for a particular location.

Figure 2.1 summarizes the basic product-selection decisions for a builder in terms of the community, product type, and product size. You must apprise the architect of each of these product decisions as well as product pricing and a summary of the target consumer expected to purchase this home or homes. If you choose an original plan, you may want to clip magazine plans, elevations, and interior features suited to the defined consumer target group to provide further guidance. Many builders keep updated files of design ideas for various consumer groups to draw upon when they are guiding architects.

Figure 2.2 illustrates an example of architect guidelines for a multiproduct community. They provide the key factors necessary for the architect to begin designing the homes. Although these guidelines are prepared for a large community, they also provide essential information guidelines for builders who need only one or two new home designs.

FIGURE 2.1   Product Selection Decisions

1. Community	2. Product Type		3. Product Size	
Type: • Center City	Multi-Family	• Elevator	No. of Bedrooms	• _____
• Urban		• Walk-up	Study, Den, Library	• _____
• Suburban	Attached	• 1 Story	No. of Bathrooms	• _____
• New		• 2 Story	No. of Dining Areas	• _____
Community		— Basement		• Dining Room
Size Total Acres				• Living Room Area
• Residential	Zero Lot Line	• 1 Story		• Kitchen Area
Development		• 2 Story		• Enclosed Terrace
• Density		— Basement	No. of Living Areas	• Inside
Parameters	Detached	• 1 Story		• Outside Covered
		• 2 Story	• Outside Uncovered	
		— Basement Parking	• Double Garage	
			• Single Garage	
			• Carport	
			• Open	

FIGURE 2.2 Sample Architect Guidelines/Product Summary

PRODUCT TYPE	LOT CONSTRAINTS	DESIGN MATRIX PRICE	SQ.FT.	$/SQ.FT	Product MIX	CONSUMER PROFILES AND CHARACTERISTICS	PRODUCT CHARACTERISTICS
1. Townhome W/Garage	Average Net Density 10 DU/ AC Lots 20'-28' Wide (interior)	88,200 97,240 102,300 106,880 111,600	1,260 1,430 1,550 1,670 1,800	70 68 66 64 62	Smallest dwellings 2 BR/ den; all others 3 BR Separate FR or Country Kitchen in two largest models. All 2-story.	Young families in child-rearing ages, single-head parent household with children, and some two-person households for family-oriented persons	Simple open floor plans with large rooms. Emphasis on square footage and family living; amenities limited to high-impact areas. Avoid temptation to overspecify. Provide basic value together with appealing design and most wanted family features.
2. Attached Patio Home (PHASE 1 – DUPLEX)	Average Net Density 6.5 DU/ AC. Lots 32'-40' for 24'-32' dwellings.	96,000 102,700 109,200 118,500 118,400	1,200 1,300 1,400 1,500 1,600	80 79 78 76 74	Smallest dwelling 2 BR then two 2 BR/Den and two 3 BR. All 1-story, although 1 1/2 (loft) okay.	Families who prefer detached SF home, but cannot afford it in this or comparable setting. Some empty nesters and single-head households	Dramatic open floor plans which capture indoor-outdoor relationships, but without expensive features normally associated with patio homes (privacy walls/fencing, atriums, decks, courtyards, etc.). Opportunity to creatively introduce lifestyle appeal within context of affordability.
3. Detached Patio Home	Average Net Density 4.5 DU/ AC. Lots 45'- 50' for 36'- 40' dwellings.	112,500 126,720 133,300 142,800 151,700	1,250 1,400 1,550 1,700 ,850	90 88 86 84 82	40% 2 BR;60% 3 BR 3 BR arranged to offer Den option. All 1-story.	Professional couples with fewer children and some empty nesters. A more sophisticated purchaser— willing to sacrifice build space for lifestyle appeal.	Dramatic open floor plans designed for entertainment/peer group appeal. Patio lifestyle apparent throughout; lots of light and interesting indoor/outdoor spacial relation- ships. Emphasis on extra amenities (wet bar, fireplace, shelves, media set-up, etc.).
4. Conventional Detached Home: Small lot	Average Net Density 4.0 DU/ AC Lots 60'- 65' for 40'-48' dwellings.	121,500 132,000 141,900 151,200 159,900	,350 ,500 ,650 ,800 ,950	90 88 86 84 82	All, at least 3 BR with family rooms larger plans can offer 4th BR or Den if practical. 2 okay for 30% plans.	Traditional family with children. Moving up for space plus up-to date features and location. Age group 25-44, but generally 40 or younger.	Value! Features are important, but extra amenities should be limited to high-impact areas. Homes must appear larger than actual sq. ft., yet rooms cannot be too open. Not a heavy entertainment group—just good family space.
5. Conventional Detached Home: Large Lot	Average Net Density 3.0 DU/ AC Lots 80' for 56'-64 dwellings.	144,000 154,000 163,400 172,200 180,400	1,600 1,750 1,900 2,050 2,200	90 88 86 84 82	60% 3 BR; 40% 3 BR Den or 4 BR/ 2-Story okay for 40% of plans, all with Family Rooms.	Second-time move-up family with children. Moving up for space and location. Move-up is somewhat reluctant. Age group 35-45.	Lots of space! Not too creative, yet offer types of space not likely to be in their current dwellings (main competition). Separate formal and informal living areas. Large break- fast areas. More compatmentalization of space but up-to-date feel.
6. Executive Home: Largest Lots in Community	Average Net Density 2.0 DU/ AC Lots 100' + for 72'-84' dwellings	162,000 176,000 189,200 201,600 213,200	1,800 2,000 2,200 2,400 2,600	90 88 86 84 82	Designs must provide for custom feature changes. Present a variety of design ideas	A show place for a small group of family consumers. The "final palace" for the breadwinner.	Spacious homes but with equal emphasis on features. Amenities should range toward the gimmicky, such as custom built-ins for stereo and TV, or intercoms, etc.

Note: New home prices vary widely across the country and over time —prices shown are for a modest price market. Dens also may be termed study, office, hobby room, etc.

The designer and builder usually interact for several weeks or even months during the design process. The more detailed your definition of a new product, the more quickly the process will proceed, particularly in the difficult concept stage. Before approving preliminary drawings and proceeding to working drawings, you should once again review all market research findings and product definition guidelines to ensure that the new product offering remains targeted to the defined consumer group. You need to make any changes now economically (on paper rather than during construction).

Street Image

Street image is the prospective buyer's initial perception of a home or community. It combines vital ingredients in product definition: landscaping, background, and the home's front facade. Poor street image may not deter a potential buyer from venturing inside, but it will certainly exert a major influence on any subsequent purchasing decisions.

Landscaping

A model home or even a speculative home must include a complete landscaping package of mature plants and trees to provide an all-important first impression on initial visitors. The often-mentioned rationale of showing each visitor exactly what is provided in the base price of the home proves unsuccessful if the visitor's first impression is negative. Do not expose yourself to unnecessary risk. Impress all visitors with the best landscaping you can offer. If the price range mandates this landscaping package be an option, inform prospects of the options on this particular model home after they are impressed with the complete house-and-lot package.

Exterior Design

While exterior design is a major part of street image, it extends beyond the facade to the other sides of the home and relates directly to the preferences of the consumer target group. You must be particularly sensitive to the aesthetic principles of exterior design and not assume that your own tastes in design are typical of each consumer target group. Please keep in mind that only a few consumer target groups exhibit characteristics and preferences similar to those of builders.

Today's builder architects and residential designers have demonstrated unprecedented excellence in creating proven exterior designs for specific consumer groups in various regions of the country. Therefore builders can fairly easily find appealing, attractive housing to construct. Because many design firms provide off-the-shelf plans targeted to specific consumer groups, individual architectural designs have become affordable for most builders. When selecting exterior design, builders must consider market research findings on consumer preferences and competitive product characteristics again. Rather than follow the leader in exterior design, you should offer distinctive new homes that incorporate the styles and external benefits and features of proven best sellers.

Efficient Floor Plans

Most consumers recognize efficient floor plans, although some builders continue to produce homes with poor floor plans. For example, the overall spaciousness of high-priced homes often disguises inefficiency. The key to ensuring efficient floor plans is to submit concept plans to a professional interior designer for hypothetical furnishing prior to creating final plans (a relatively inexpensive assignment). With scale furniture in place, circulation and space problems become apparent.

Figure 2.3 illustrates the potential of incorporating distinctive features in every room of a builder's home. This prototype floor plan by nationally known residential architects Bloodgood Sharp Buster combines the best features of many plans to indicate optimum potential for broad consumer appeal. Adapt some or all of these ideas to improve the marketability of your next model home.

Special Features

Essential to high sales absorption, special features vary in number and quality depending upon the price of the home. However, every new home, no matter how small, should contain special features to attract consumers, particularly in high-impact kitchens and bathrooms. For example, special features in bathrooms and kitchens might include the ones in the following lists:

Special Bathroom Features

- double lavatory in vanity and make-up knee space
- tub as focal point from entry, with glass as a backdrop
- vaulted or raised ceilings with plant shelves above closets
- transom glass windows above mirrors over lavatories
- compartmentalized or camouflaged water closet
- exercise area in—or adjacent to—the bath
- columns to define views
- his-and-hers closets (in markets where consumers accept integrated closets and bathrooms)
- dressing areas
- shower adjacent to tub with glass enclosure

Special Kitchen Features

- walk-in pantry
- breakfast nook directly adjacent to kitchen
- vaulted or raised ceilings with plant shelves above cabinets
- island cabinets
- sink placed for panoramic view of the outdoors, either through family room or windows
- flush cabinetry with appliances that blend into and virtually become part of the cabinets
- pass-through counters from kitchen to dining areas
- location adjacent to family room with minimal distance to garage

FIGURE 2.3   Bloodgood Sharp Buster Plan

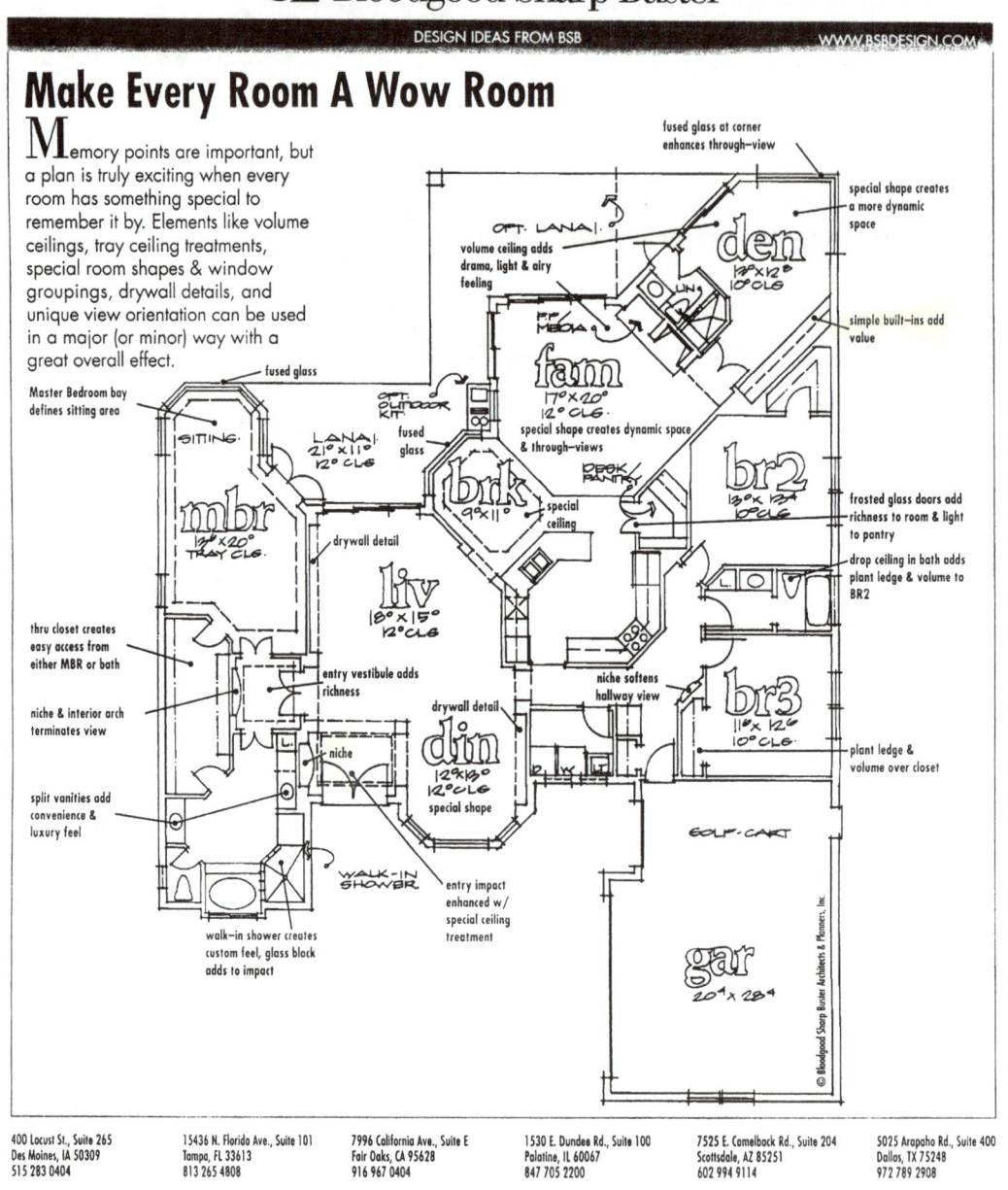

Architects and Planners, Inc.
Bloodgood Sharp Buster
DESIGN IDEAS FROM BSB   WWW.BSBDESIGN.COM

Make Every Room A Wow Room

Memory points are important, but a plan is truly exciting when every room has something special to remember it by. Elements like volume ceilings, tray ceiling treatments, special room shapes & window groupings, drywall details, and unique view orientation can be used in a major (or minor) way with a great overall effect.

Labels on plan:
- fused glass at corner enhances through-view
- special shape creates a more dynamic space
- volume ceiling adds drama, light & airy feeling
- simple built-ins add value
- fused glass
- Master Bedroom bay defines sitting area
- frosted glass doors add richness to room & light to pantry
- drop ceiling in bath adds plant ledge & volume to BR2
- fused glass
- special ceiling
- drywall detail
- thru closet creates easy access from either MBR or bath
- niche & interior arch terminates view
- entry vestibule adds richness
- niche softens hallway view
- drywall detail
- niche
- plant ledge & volume over closet
- split vanities add convenience & luxury feel
- entry impact enhanced w/ special ceiling treatment
- walk-in shower creates custom feel, glass block adds to impact

Room labels on plan:
- OPT. LANAI
- den 13°x12° 10° CLG
- fam 17°x20° 12° CLG
- LANAI 21°x11° 12° CLG
- brk 9°x11°
- br2 13°x13° 10° CLG
- mbr 13°x20° TRAY CLG
- SITTING
- liv 18°x15° 12° CLG
- br3 11°x12° 10° CLG
- din 12°x13° 12° CLG special shape
- WALK-IN SHOWER
- GOLF-CART
- gar 20°x28°
- OPT. OUTDOOR KIT
- DRY PANTRY

© Bloodgood Sharp Buster Architects & Planners, Inc.

400 Locust St., Suite 265
Des Moines, IA 50309
515 283 0404

15436 N. Florida Ave., Suite 101
Tampa, FL 33613
813 265 4808

7996 California Ave., Suite E
Fair Oaks, CA 95628
916 967 0404

1530 E. Dundee Rd., Suite 100
Palatine, IL 60067
847 705 2200

7525 E. Camelback Rd., Suite 204
Scottsdale, AZ 85251
602 994 9114

5025 Arapaho Rd., Suite 400
Dallas, TX 75248
972 789 2908

Courtesy of Bloodgood Sharp Buster Architects and Planners, Inc., Des Moines, Iowa

When considering these features, you should keep in mind that everyone wants to feel special, and every new home prospect will respond positively to features suited to his or her preferences.

Due Diligence

Due diligence is a legal term for actions taken by real estate developers and builders prior to land purchase to avoid liability. It generally includes market scale and growth, consumer characteristics, competitor characteristics, and development constraints (physical, legal, and political). These elements serve as a basis for revenue projection followed by a financial pro forma (plan of annual revenues and expenses). Completing all the analysis steps in Chapter 1 will provide you with every requirement for a due diligence report if an investor or lender requests one.

According to planner David Jensen, "A thorough understanding of regulatory, contextual, and market forces which impact a particular site is vital to successful development . . . Purchasing raw land without doing adequate research can doom the project before it starts."

Builders requiring only a few lots at a single location may assume that the land developer is responsible for such due diligence—an assumption often leading to unnecessary problems. Make no assumptions about necessary research on your site-selection decisions, regardless of scale. Make sure it is completed to your satisfaction according to the evaluation guidelines in this chapter.

3

Prepare the Strategic Marketing Plan

Every residential development is preceded by planning, whether by accident or design. The goal of strategic planning is to achieve the best revenues through cost-effective marketing techniques that attract target consumers to the site where you impress them with a high-quality presentation in support of the selling process.

Figure 3.1 summarizes the strategic planning process for new homes marketing. It begins with market research input described in Chapter 1: (a) consumer demand for new homes and (b) a competitive supply of new homes products to meet that demand are related to (c) development constraints on a site identified for new products defined according to the three preceding factors. This research is the basis for the three phases of the strategic marketing plan.

Strategy

The marketing strategy is the formula for achieving marketing objectives. It defines product positioning and the consumer market for achieving projected consumer inquiries, site visitors, and dwelling sales.

Product Positioning
Positioning ensures that the product offering and its marketing description suit the targeted consumers' needs and preferences. Positioning influences the mind of your consumer through the product presentation and marketing messages. It is the distinctive images or ideas retained by consumers about the product offerings that some marketers refer to as the unique selling proposition.

FIGURE 3.1 Strategic Planning Process

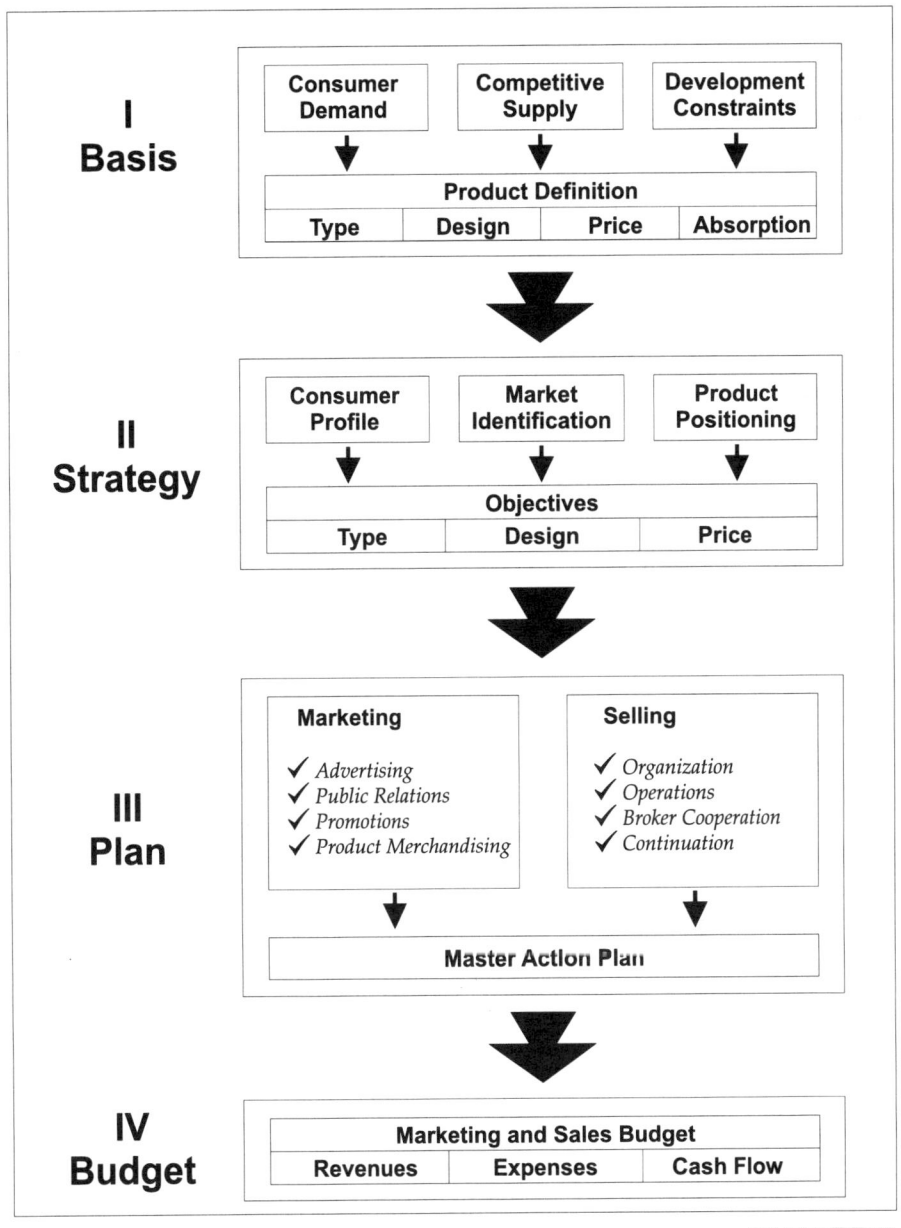

MARKETING AND SALES
PLANNING AND BUDGETING

I
Basis

Consumer Demand	Competitive Supply	Development Constraints

Product Definition

Type	Design	Price	Absorption

II
Strategy

Consumer Profile	Market Identification	Product Positioning

Objectives

Type	Design	Price

III
Plan

Marketing
- ✓ Advertising
- ✓ Public Relations
- ✓ Promotions
- ✓ Product Merchandising

Selling
- ✓ Organization
- ✓ Operations
- ✓ Broker Cooperation
- ✓ Continuation

Master Action Plan

IV
Budget

Marketing and Sales Budget		
Revenues	Expenses	Cash Flow

PARKER98
ASSOCIATES

Successful builders recognize the vital importance of positioning. They understand that a well-designed and well-constructed product presented with attractive merchandising is not sufficient to achieve adequate sales. However, in the increasingly competitive markets, you need to make a special impression in the minds of consumers, minds that already are subjected to information overload from many sources including competitive builders. You must compress your information into small messages in the style of the most popular news magazines and national newspapers. Simplicity is mandatory, and the message must focus on emotional rather than rational associations. You must communicate an especially memorable image that is distinct from any images your potential home buyers may have retained from competitive products.

You can confirm positioning by preparing a profile of targeted consumer groups for the proposed dwellings and list the key positioning factors (dwelling benefits and features and community amenities). These factors provide guidelines for architectural design. They also serve as the subsequent criteria for selecting the best designs for your consumers and the best ways of presenting model dwellings to appeal to these consumers.

Chapter 1 defined various types of consumer groups with respect to needs and preferences for specific types of product offerings. The special positioning of these offerings to one or more of these consumer groups is the essential first step in strategic marketing.

Figure 3.2 provides a sample summary table for organizing positioning factors of a product—community and dwellings—to the eight primary consumer groups:

- couples and singles under age 45
  - singles and tandems
  - young couples
- couples and singles over age 45
  - singles and tandems
  - empty nester couples
  - retiree couples
- families with children
  - single parents
  - one-income couples
  - two-income couples

Tandems are two or more nonconjugal persons living together for economic or companionship reasons. *Empty nester* couples include one or both persons employed in primary occupations as differentiated from retiree couples who no longer are employed in primary occupations. The profile split at age 45 recognizes a lifestyle watershed after which persons tend to have established family, occupation, income, and interest patterns that shape their housing decisions. Families with children transcend the age-45 watershed in terms of housing needs and preferences.

The community amenities and dwelling features listed in Figure 3.2 serve as samples to help you to select the key influences for your primary target consumers,

FIGURE 3.2 Product Positioning Summary

	Under Age 45		Over Age 45			Families/Kids		
	Singles Tandems	Young Couples	Singles Tandems	Empty Nesters	Retired Couples	Single Parents	1 Income Couples	2 Income Couples
CHARACTERISTICS								
Household Size								
Age: Adults								
Children								
Income								
Lifestyle (code)								
COMMUNITY AMENITIES								
Recreation:								
Pool								
Tennis								
Golf								
Playground								
Playfields								
Park								
Boating								
Indoor Recreation								
Club								
Other								
Shopping:								
Convenience Shopping								
Specialty Shopping								
Schools:								
Elementary								
Secondary								
Other:								
Civic Library Fire/EMT Police								
DWELLING FEATURES								
Kitchen:								
Microwave								
Ice Maker								
Disposal								
Compactor								
Washer/Dryer								
Bathroom:								
Whirlpool tub								
Separate shower								
Double vanity								
Extra linen closet								
Living:								
Fireplace								
Wet bar								
Entertainment center								
Built-ins								
Volume Ceilings								
Special flooring								
Den/Study/Office								
Exterior:								
Garage (1,2,3)								
Patio/balcony								
Enclosed patio/balcony								
Hot tub								
Special landscape								

the list is not intended to be comprehensive. From these key influences, you must define the unique selling proposition that will set your product apart from competition and thereby constitute the optimum positioning for marketing your new homes. Some marketers refer to this positioning as establishing a brand or trademark. It gives you a special signature that consumers in your marketplace can remember. Like a signature, positioning must be simple and distinctive to survive in the crowded memories of your consumers.

Consumer Market

The marketplace for your new homes development is defined properly as two markets: One delineates the area in which potential consumers now live and a second delineates the area encompassing your major competitors. The consumer market area is often much larger than the competitive market area. For example, a suburban new homes community may successfully attract consumers from throughout a metropolitan area, but the major competitors may be clustered in a single school district in one segment of the metropolitan area.

Figure 3.3 illustrates this dual-market concept in the Atlanta metropolitan area. Purchasers of new homes in a development in suburban Forsyth County came from an area extending into the central city, whereas primary competitors are located within a radius of 10 miles of the site. The consumer market encompasses parts of six counties and the competitive market is entirely within one county.

Retirees and purchasers of vacation homes often come from dispersed distant markets that require costly definition, legal registration fees for individual states, and special marketing communications to persuade inquiring consumers to become site visitors. The competitive market for these products also is likely to be more dispersed than for primary homes because competitive communities often are spread across many counties or even states.

In determining your consumer market, you also should examine the potentially significant submarkets within the market area. Such submarkets may be appropriate for cost-effective communication through neighborhood newspapers, direct mail, or personal-interaction programs. These segments within the overall market may reveal opportunities for special sponsoring promotional events such as charity sports events and hosting a party in a major rental apartment complex.

As sales progress, you may discover particular neighborhoods from which several purchasers originated. Such cases present opportunities for targeting these neighborhood submarkets through both advertising and referral programs in which you motivate your purchasers to refer former neighbors as prospective neighbors in one of your new homes.

Marketing Objectives

You must support your sales objectives for monthly and annual performance with marketing objectives in terms of consumer inquiries and site visitors who become prospective purchasers. Marketing performance can only be evaluated by—and sales can only be made to—identified prospects. Approximations of visitor traffic to your site are useless statistics without information about each visitor for follow-up activities.

FIGURE 3.3 Dual Market Concept

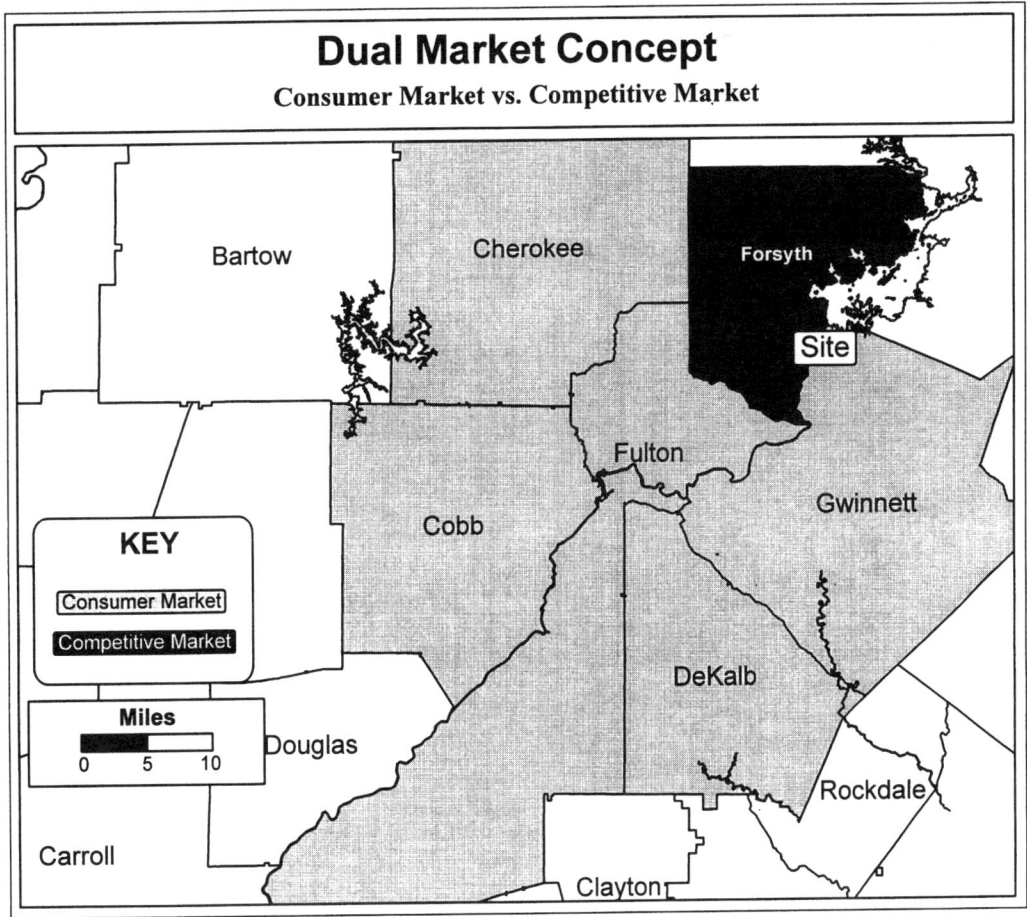

Dual Market Concept
Consumer Market vs. Competitive Market

KEY

Consumer Market
Competitive Market

Miles
0   5   10

Bartow

Cherokee

Forsyth

Site

Fulton

Gwinnett

Cobb

DeKalb

Douglas

Rockdale

Carroll

Clayton

Sales Objectives. Contrary to the oft-quoted opinions of some builders, appraisers, analysts, and marketers, sales absorption does not occur at a constant rate throughout a particular development (for example, four sales per month). Although special market conditions, marketing campaigns, and gifted sales people, can stimulate sales absorption, the greatest influence on the rate of sales is development progress. Consumers tend to buy what they see, and developments that are more mature in terms of completed infrastructure, amenities, and new homes generally sell at a faster rate than those in the pioneer stage of little or partial completion of these components. Happy residents generate more happy residents.

Therefore you should define sales objectives in harmony with your development schedule—at an increasing rate as your development matures. Make your goals consistent with previous experience with a similar development. Unless you are fortunate enough to be in a market where consumer demand vastly exceeds new home supply, sales contracted prior to completion of model homes will be relatively few compared to sales contracted after completion of initial infrastructure, amenities, and resident occupancy. Once a neighborhood achieves over 50-percent occupancy, sales absorption should reach its peak, and it usually declines during the final phase of a development as lot selections become more limited. A decline in sales absorption usually occurs within 85 to 90 percent of a development's sellout.

Figure 3.4 illustrates the normal distribution of sales for a new home neighborhood of 100 or more homes.

Marketing Objectives. Marketing objectives should relate to sales objectives in terms of a growth curve similar to the sales absorption curve in Figure 3.4. Because selling new homes from plans is more difficult than selling completed models, your sales conversion rate—number of consumer inquiries per sale—is usually lower in the predevelopment and initial development stages of a neighborhood, or even an individual model home, than it is after the development has achieved the mature stage described above. You may require as many or more consumer inquiries, but the lower sales conversion rate will generate fewer sales than at development maturity.

Figure 3.5 summarizes sales and marketing objectives for a planned development of 300 new homes in the Sunbelt (year-round building construction) in which virtually all consumer inquiries are site visitors (a normal primary home builder situation) rather than phone, mail, or e-mail inquiries. In this example the 300 homes were sold in 3.5 years, an average of 7.1 sales per month, but only 66 sales were achieved in the first 15 months for an average of 4.4 sales per month until development maturity. During this same 15-month period of predevelopment and initial development selling, 1,900 consumer inquiries produced an average sales conversion rate of 3.5 percent. During the subsequent mature

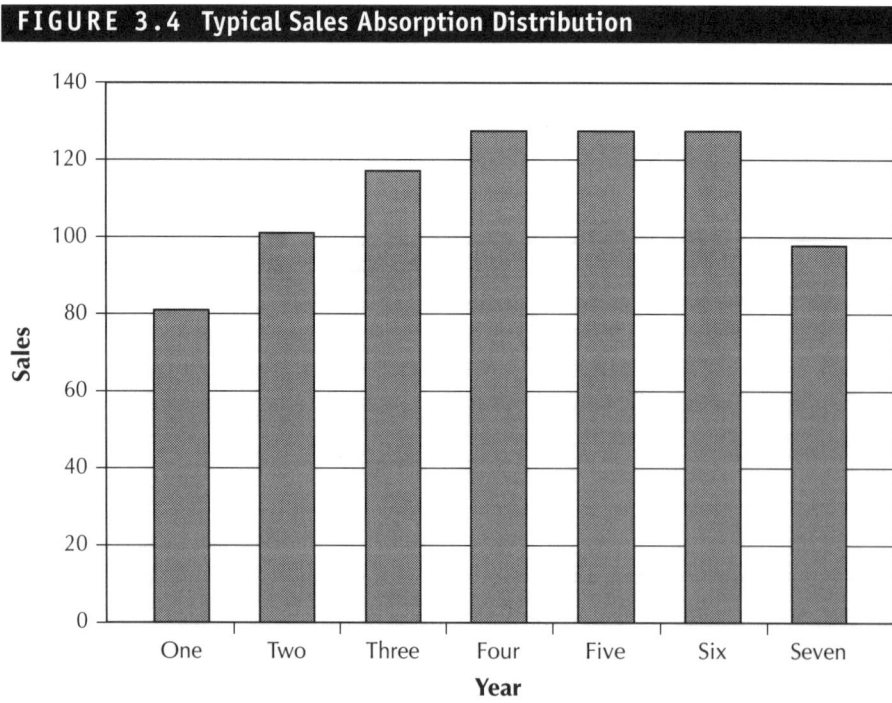

FIGURE 3.4 Typical Sales Absorption Distribution

FIGURE 3.5 Summary of Sales and Marketing Objectives

Stage	Quarter	Sales	Percent	Conversion	Inquiries	Percent
Pre	1	9		3.0%	300	
Development	2	12		3.0	400	
Sub total		**21**	**7**		**700**	**13**
Initial	3	12		3.0	400	
Development	4	15		3.8	400	
	5	18		4.5	400	
Subtotal		**45**	**15**		**1,200**	**22**
	6	21		5.2	400	
Mature	7	27		6.7	400	
Development	8	30		7.5	400	
	9	30		7.5	400	
	10	30		7.5	400	
	11	30		7.5	400	
	12	30		7.5	400	
Sub total		**198**	**66**		**2,800**	**51**
Final	13	21		5.2	400	
Development	14	15		3.8	400	
Sub total		**36**	**12**		**800**	**15**
Total	**14**	**300**	**100**	**5.5%**	**5,500**	**100**

development stage, 198 sales resulted from 2,800 inquiries at an average sales conversion rate of over 7 percent. Thus, assuming each consumer inquiry requires the same cost, marketing a mature development is twice as cost-effective as marketing a development before maturity.

This example responds to the often-asked question of why not increase marketing exposure in the predevelopment and initial development stages to increase sales? The answer is that you probably can increase sales during these stages, but at double the marketing cost per sale compared to marketing costs in the mature stage of development. Perhaps a better question is why not defer marketing and sales operations until development infrastructure, initial amenities, and models are complete? The answer is that you probably can achieve sellout in almost the same overall time period at much lower costs. But few developers and builders appear to have the patience to save these predevelopment costs and improve their profit margins accordingly.

Consumer Attraction Costs. The marketing costs for generating consumers for new homes are often referred to as consumer attraction costs. They include advertising, publicity, and promotion to communicate with consumers. For retirement and resort communities that must respond to phone, mail, and Internet inquiries to convert consumers to site visitors, these attraction costs are much higher than for primary home communities that attract consumers directly to the site. In general a builder selling popularly priced homes can expect to spend about one-tenth of 1 percent of the sales price of a house for each consumer inquiry generated. For example, if your average sales price is $125,000 in an average-cost media market, you can plan to spend about $125 per site visitor on consumer attraction. Higher-priced products offered by builders and developers of resort communities may spend double that amount per consumer inquiry. Small-volume builders may reduce their marketing costs by purchasing lots in a community marketed by the developer or by relying upon real estate agents to market their homes. However, such cost savings usually require relinquishing marketing decisions to others.

Merchandising Costs. The costs for site marketing signs, information centers, model home décor, sales support brochures, and other collateral information are referred to as merchandizing costs. They are not related directly to consumer generation, although they tend to be higher for high-volume traffic locations. Merchandising costs are somewhat discretionary with respect to consumer inquiry generation. Generally you should plan costs for each development according to the merchandising needs of a particular property and the number of builders involved. As a general rule, you should plan for merchandising costs of 1 to 2 percent of projected sales revenues over $10 million and a higher ratio for revenues below this level.

Therefore, in the example of 300 homes sales in Figure 3.5, an average selling price of $125,000 per home would generate $37.5 million in sales revenues of which $375,000 to $750,000 (average $562,500) would be anticipated for merchandising costs (1 to 2 percent). Consumer attraction costs of $125 per inquiry for 5,500 inquiries would add about $700,000. Thus the example would incur total marketing costs of approximately $1.3 million or about 3.5 percent of total sales revenues. This marketing percentage could be lower for larger-scale properties or for builders operating in a planned community with developer marketing, and it could be higher for relatively low-volume developments of, for example, less than 75 popular priced homes on an independent site.

Marketing Plan

Your marketing plan should include selling components for organization (including compensation policies), operations, real estate agent cooperation, and purchaser satisfaction plus five interrelated marketing components: identity creation, public relations, promotions, advertising, and merchandising. These components are equally applicable to designing a marketing plan for a specific development of any size or for a home builder with a multilocation operation. Organizing the five components into a unified development or annual marketing plan requires you to identify cost-effectiveness guidelines for consumer attraction and merchandising requirements for your particular application.

Selling Components

Selling components often are relegated to a simple budget percentage of revenues and assumed to be managed efficiently by a sales director. A detailed plan for these selling components is not part of this book, except to provide planning guidelines.

Organizing a new homes sales team requires establishing sales policies and procedures and distributing them in a manual or three-ring binder for consistent application by all of your staff. This manual explains the size of staff required and their compensation requirements in addition to providing details of every aspect of the selling process. Such a manual requires a minimum of 3 months to complete by professional staff. Based on the sales policies manual, operations can commence by first hiring and preparing the sales team and then ensuring their success through a uniform sales education program. Initiating these sales operations, including implementing a performance evaluation system and management reports, requires an initial 2 months of which half can overlap with preparing the sales policies manual. Implementing a real estate agent cooperation program and a purchaser satisfaction program extend into the selling process past initial resident occupancy.

Marketing Components

The five marketing components are described in detail through subsequent chapters of this book. Your marketing plan requires summarizing activities for each component throughout the time period of the plan. You should implement these components according to cost-effectiveness criteria for each component to generate the number of consumer inquiries required to achieve sales objectives for the least cost.

For example, if your market analysis indicates realistic sales objectives of 24 the first year, 30 the second year, and 36 the third year, and if your sales team can convert an average of 7 percent of all visitor prospects into purchasers, you need a plan for attracting 343 prospects in the first year, 429 prospects the second year, and 514 prospects the third year (sales objectives divided by conversion rate). If you estimate the sales team will only convert 4 percent of prospects to purchasers, then you must generate 600 prospects during the first year to achieve 24 sales.

The most economical means of generating these prospects are the essence of the marketing plan. Appealing site and model merchandising and other selling support elements follow them. Most successful marketing plans coordinate a mixture of various advertising media and public relations activities. How much of each type of media you use depends on the cost-effectiveness experience in your market. Many local builders rely upon newspaper advertising and outdoor signs (both billboards and roadside trailblazers), whereas others find additional media to be cost-effective, such as targeted direct mail, new home consumer magazines, radio and television (particularly for special promotion events). Some of them also rely on a local real estate agent.

You should track the cost of each of these media relative to the number of prospects attributed to this source by asking each visitor how he or she learned about your site. By this means you can calculate the cost of each prospect inquiry according to the number of inquiries attributable to specific costs of advertising. For example, a newspaper advertising program cost $5,000 for 1 month, and during that time, it generated 40 inquiries. That source would have a cost effectiveness of $125 per inquiry. If the sales conversion rate is 7 percent, the advertising cost per sale from this source is $1,786 ($5,000/.07 × 40).

However, just as you provide a variety of new home plans to suit variable consumer tastes so must you utilize a number of advertising media to reach consumers who may not respond to your most cost-effective medium. The blending of these media for generating prospects over several months could be accomplished by using the following master action program.

Master Action Program

The master action program is a detailed schedule of priorities and timing for each component of the marketing plan. Figure 3.6 provides a bar chart for a typical master action program designed for a new homes development. It clearly indicates the time requirements for each of the foregoing elements in a development, and the plan calls for the visitor center and model home to be completed the first week of March. The builder has decided to heed the advice of his marketing consultant and coordinate the start of sales operations with completion of merchandising (rather than using the common inefficient practice of attempting to sell from a temporary location on the construction site).

FIGURE 3.6 Launch Campaign Master Action Program

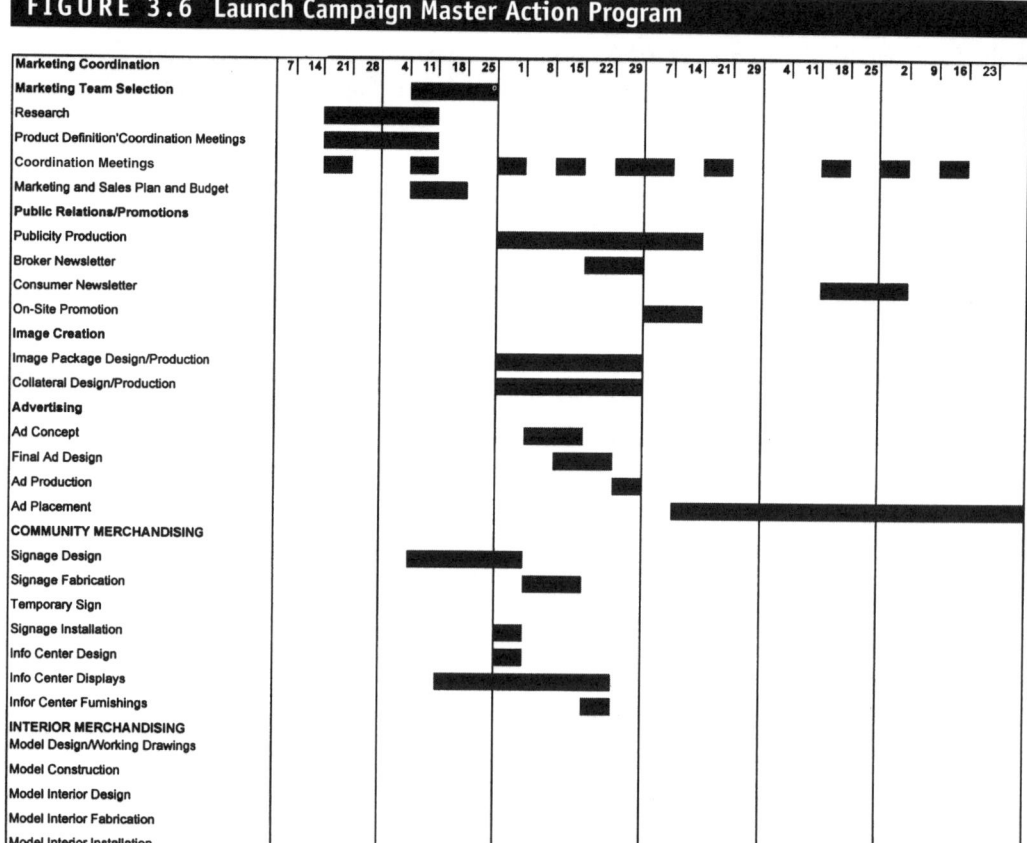

Planning for an optimum marketing launch campaign must begin at least 3 months prior to the scheduled opening of the model with an update of market research to confirm consumer preferences and product definition (offerings and prices). After that update, you should prepare the budget and select all marketing and sales team members. Team coordination meetings begin and participation increases as you select new team members.

Public relations activities include producing publicity on team members and product offerings, plus human interest articles about the site, for release before and after the model opening. A newsletter for real estate agents informs all local agents about this offering prior to opening. (The consumer newsletter is deferred for follow-up distribution to initial prospects.) You need to plan on-site promotions for the model opening and the real estate preview especially if you can involve political and financial persons important to the development's success.

Your team members need to translate the identity of the development into an image package, collateral brochures, and selling support information and coordinate it with preparation of advertising for placement during the week prior to model opening. Community merchandising must be designed and completed prior to opening to fully complement the model home, and the visitor information center must be designed with specific environment and informational displays. The model merchandiser customarily requires 3 months to design, fabricate, and install interior décor.

You should review the marketing master action program monthly when launching a new development to ensure that all marketing elements are on target and coordinated with model home construction. If construction delays occur, corresponding changes in marketing schedules should reduce unnecessary advance expenditures. Conversely, accelerated construction may require creative shortcuts to ensure that marketing elements are in place for a timely launch.

Marketing Budget

Your marketing budget should provide cost estimates of activities under each of the marketing plan components in relation to total, or annual, sales revenue projections. Separating sales support costs from the cost of attracting customers will allow you to calculate them in terms of cost per inquiry to evaluate marketing performance, marketing management, merchandising. You can then compare the cost per inquiry for alternative advertising and public relations programs to select the most cost-effective program.

Establishing a workable planned budget requires, among other items, an operational business plan, a monthly schedule of starts, sales, and settlements, along with an understanding of all the line-item expenditures required by the marketing operation. Most important of all, do not forget to prepare, update, and review a monthly cash flow forecast covering at least the next 12 months. Remember, to understand the business, you must understand your numbers.

FIGURE 3.7 Marketing Budget Summary

	Sub-totals	Totals	Percent
Control		____	____
Research		____	____
Performance Evaluation		____	____
Planning Budgeting		____	____
Marketing Administration	____	____	
CONSUMER ATTRACTION		$____	____
Public Relations		$____	____
Agency Fees	____		
Publicity Production	____		
Promotions	$____		
On-site Promotions	____		
Off-site Promotions	$____		
Promotion Production	____		
Advertising		$____	____
Newspaper	$____		
Magazines	____		
Radio/TV	____		
Outdoor Signs	____		
Direct Mail	____		
Internet Website	____		
Ad Agency Fees	____		
Advertising Production	____		
SELLING SUPPORT		$____	____
Identity Creation		____	____
Design	$____		
Collaterals	____		
Merchandising		$____	____
Site Signs	$____		
Information Center Design	____		
Information Center Displays	____		
Information Center Operations	____		
Models Interior Design	____		
Models Operations	____		
Landscaping	____		
Total		$____	100
Estimated Revenue		____	
Percent of Revenue		____	

Figure 3.7 presents a marketing budget summary for a single development or time period. It contains estimates of expenditures for each of the marketing components described above. It is divided into control, consumer attraction, and selling support for easy monitoring. As noted above, you should first provide a control total for consumer attraction by estimating prospect objectives in terms of cost per inquiry.

Control and selling support costs must be estimated for each line item and then evaluated with respect to share of total revenues. Depending on whether your costs are shared with a land developer, resort operation, or other builders, your total marketing costs should average 2 to 4 percent of total new home revenues.

Budgeting Guidelines

Consumer attraction costs—public relations and advertising—are sensitive to the rate of sales absorption. They can expand or contract substantially if sales absorption is below or above projections. Therefore reliable budgeting depends upon realistic sales absorption projections varied according to season and development maturity because new homes sell better in some seasons. They also sell better as a development matures, up until the diminishing amount of product available limits sales).

Reliable budgeting depends upon rejecting the commonly held myth that marketing is directly proportional to revenues. As noted above, marketing costs are much higher at the beginning of a development to establish selling support. Some locations and products also require proportionately higher consumer attraction costs than others. You should reject rule-of-thumb budget estimating and treat each new development as a unique selling situation requiring a budget constructed of individually estimated line items.

Budgeting for Consumer Attraction

In estimating costs for public relations, promotions, and advertising, you should first obtain a control total by multiplying consumer inquiry objectives by historic cost-per-inquiry data. If company records are insufficient to supply cost per inquiry data, you can apply a trial control total. Use a range of $100 to $250 per inquiry depending on market demand and supply as well as on-site location factors (and in some metropolitan areas, higher-than-average costs for advertising production and placement).

Within the parameters of the control total, allocate expenditures first to relatively constant public relations and promotions costs and then to variable advertising costs. These expenditures, of course, must cover the entire marketing period determined by your projection of sales absorption.

For example, publicity is best generated by a public relations specialist on a monthly retainer or a periodic per diem (plus direct expenses). In either case this expenditure remains constant through sellout (or annually). Newsletters and promotions are also budgeted as constant costs per time period. Once these constraints are estimated per time period, a straightforward calculation will give you a total public relations and promotions budget.

Subtracting expenditures for public relations and promotions from the above-listed control total provides an overall advertising budget total. Allocating this total through sellout (or annually) requires knowing local media rates and making trial distributions to determine the adequacy of expenditures (or a possible surplus) to ensure regular media exposure. These trial distributions involve decision-making similar to determining standard features for a home. You must balance strong consumer appeal and cost-effectiveness. Figure 3.8 is an advertising budget worksheet for a small residential development.

FIGURE 3.8 Advertising Budgeting Worksheet

1998	Times-Union	Jax Mag	Jax Mthly	Outdoor	Total
May	8 1/2 p ads $14,000	FC ad $1,200	FC ad $12,000	$28,400	$28,400
June	8 1/4 p ads 7,000	—	—	—	7,000
July	5 1/8 p ads 2,200		—	—	2,200
Aug	4 1/8 p ads 1,800	—	—	—	1,800
Sept	5 1/4 p ads 4,400	FC ad 1,200	FC ad 1,200	—	6,800
Oct	8 1/4 p ads 7,000	FC ad 1,200	FC ad 1,200	—	9,400
Nov	4 1/8 p ads 1,800	—	—	—	1,800
1998 Total	47 ads 40,400	3ads 3,600	3,600	12,000	59,600
1999	4,500	4,800	4,800	12,000	66,600
2000	45,000	4,800	4,800	12,000	66,600
2001	45,000	4,800	4,800	12,000	66,600
2002	45,000	4,800	4,800	12,000	66,600
2003	35,000	3,600	3,600		42,200
2004	35,000	3,600	3,600		42,200
2005	35,000	3,600	3,600		42,200
Total	$325,400	$33,600	$33,600	$60,000	$425,600

Budgeting for Product Merchandising

Product merchandising expenditures include three major components:

- identity creation (also vital to public relations and advertising)
- community or site merchandising
- interior or model merchandising

Regardless of the scale of expenditures for each of these components, you must examine each for positive impact on the selling process, and establish priorities for budget trade-off. Consumer attraction expenditures tend to be distributed throughout the selling period, but generally you must budget for merchandising expenditures at the beginning of the development. Therefore merchandising expenditures are virtually all front-end negative cash flow (except for possible brochure reprints and refurbishing models for developments selling beyond 3 years).

Furniture Costs. Many professional merchandisers now provide optional leased furniture. Purchased furniture costs can be partially recovered depending on the duration of model use. The following are general guidelines for model furnishings cost recovery:

Model Years	Cost Recovery
1	60%
2	40
3	30
4	25
5	10–20

Sample Budget

Figure 3.9 provides a sample marketing budget for a small development that shows the importance of distributing expenses through to sellout in order to plan cash flow.

FIGURE 3.9 Sample Marketing Budget

Sales Revenues $14,800,000	Expenses	Sub Total	Total	Percent %	1998	1998	1999	1999	1999	1999	2000	2000	2000	2000	2001
I. CONTROL			72.0	0.49											
Marketing Coordintation	56				5.0	9.0	9.0	9.0	6.0	6.0	6.0	2.0	2.0	2.0	
Travel & Expenses	16				0.2	0.2	1.8	1.8	1.8	1.8	1.8	1.6	1.6	1.6	
II. MARKET			281.5	1.90											
Agency Costs		63.8													
Fees	53.5				4.0	`10.5	`10.5	`10.5	6.0	6.0	6.0				
Travel & Expenses	10.3				2.0	2.3	1.5	0.7	0.8	0.7					
Public Relations		31													
Consumer Newsletter	10.0					2.5	2.5		2.5		2.5				
Broker Nesletter	9					1.5	1.5	1.5	1.5		1.5	1.5			
Photography	12						1.0	1.0		1.0					
Promotions	17					5.0	5.0	1.0	1.0	1.0	1.0	1.0	1.0	1.0	1.0
Advertising		169.7					5.4	4.1	1.5	0.5	4.1	1.5	1.5	0.5	
Magazine	19.1						24.0	12.0	12.0	12.0	12.0	12.0	12.0	12.0	12.0
Newspaper	120							5.4	5.4	5.4	5.4				
Billboards	21.6					2.0									
Other Signs	2					0.0									
Direct Mail	0														
Production	7					5.0				1.0		1.0			
III. PRODUCT MERCHANDISING			91.0	0.61											
Image	3.0					3.0									
Signs	8.0						8.0								
Info Ctr. Design															
Info Ctr. Construction	10.0						10.0								
Info Ctr. Displays	15.0					7.5	7.5								
Model Interior	50.0					25.0	25.0								
Mont Int. Recovery	-10.0														-10.0
Colaterals	15					15.0									
IV. Sell			380.4	2.57											
Direct Sales Costs		262.5				7.5	10.2	11.0	12.0	10.5	10.5	12.0	12.0	7.5	6.0
Sales commissions		99.2				10.0	17.0	17.0	17.0	17.0	17.0	17.0	17.0	17.0	17.0
Realtor Commissions		162.0					0.4	0.4	0.4	0.4	0.4	0.4	0.4	0.4	0.4
Owner Gists		3.3													
Indirect Sales Csts		117.9													
Sales Salaries		50.0				5.0	5.0	5.0	5.0	5.0	5.0	5.0	5.0	5.0	5.0
Operating Expanses		12.5					2.5	2.5	2.5	2.5	2.5	2.5			
Benefits		36.0				3.6	3.6	3.6	3.6	3.6	3.6	3.6	3.6	3.6	3.6
		19.4				1.5	1.8	2.2	2.3	2.2	2.2	2.3	2.0	1.5	1.4
Total	824.9		824.9	5.57	20.2	117.9	115.2	88.5	82.2	75.7	83.2	62.4	59.1	52.1	32.4

In this example, total marketing expenses for each time period are compared with projected revenues to clearly separate front-end marketing costs.

Selecting Marketing Specialists

Although some builders undertake marketing functions in-house, most builders who are expanding their businesses retain public relations, advertising, and merchandising specialists who interact as a marketing team under the direction of the builder's marketing executive. Proven means of locating talent, selecting marketing team members, and team communication guidelines are discussed in the following paragraphs.

Many builders adopt a team approach to designing and marketing new offerings. These builders bring the same group of outside specialists together with key staff for planning each new development. Repetitive interaction leads to efficient synergistic relationships as well as economic fees for the outside specialists. A marketing team typically consists of the following specialists:

- marketing/research consultant
- land planner/landscape architect
- architect
- model merchandiser
- public relations/promotions agency
- advertising agency
- graphics designer

Marketing/Research Consultant

Marketing consultants can provide builders with a variety of services, beginning with initial feasibility or market research and continuing through final sellout. You may choose continuous service from marketing specialists or use them only periodically for specific work. At a minimum every builder needs the results of market research to provide creative direction to other marketing team members.

Land Planner and/or Landscape Architect

After research has been completed, the land planner is usually the first marketing team member to begin work. Because land planning decisions affect architectural design at a later stage, the architect should review preliminary land plans to ensure optimum coordination and design results.

Principal or Partner. The principal of a firm controls both the creative direction and daily activity of the company. Depending upon the size of the firm and complexity of the development, this individual may also function as the chief planner.

Senior Planner. In a large firm a senior planner assumes day-to-day responsibility for developing preliminary concepts, "bubble" diagrams, or sketches. Once you approve the concepts, the senior planner oversees refining concept drawings into detailed working plans.

Staff Planner. A staff planner is a less experienced professional who works under the creative direction of a senior planner or partner to develop concepts and refine them into working plans.

Architect

Land planning and architectural design are interrelated—the opportunities and limitations of each affect the other. Large architectural firms routinely provide land planning as part of their services to ensure harmony in the design of land and homes. The key members of an architectural team are described in the following paragraphs.

Principal or Partner. The principals work directly with the builder to assess architectural needs and define the scope of work. They oversee all work and provide creative direction for each account.

Director of Design. The creative process of design translates research information and target consumer profiles into appropriately designed new homes. The director, usually someone with a strong marketing background, schedules work and provides creative direction to the department staff.

Director of Production. Once designs are completed and approved, the production department develops full working drawings and specifications for each new home. The director schedules work and reviews all plans for completeness, accuracy, and appropriateness of the specifications to the plan and to the target market.

Senior Architect. A senior architect is assigned to each architectural project. Assisted by staff architects and draftspersons, the senior architect is responsible for the overall design and production of finished drawings.

Model Merchandiser

Model merchandising is an important marketing tool for builders. Model homes should not simply be furnished by a local furniture store decorator; they should be merchandised by a professional with skill and experience in new home marketing. A model merchandising firm typically assigns a team to each model or model series.

Principal or Partner. The principal is responsible for (a) the creative concept that integrates the marketing profile with architectural plans and the community theme, (b) key design choices, and (c) builder-merchandiser contact.

Senior Designer. The senior designer (a) works with the builder on day-to-day coordination of merchandising efforts; (b) implements the creative concept through specification and purchasing; (c) supervises field coordination, subcontracted work, and installation.

Installation Crew. Under the direction of the senior designer, the installation crew installs all furniture and decorator items in the model.

Public Relations/Promotions Agency

The public relations/promotions specialist with whom the builder works is usually either a company principal or senior representative. The nature of public relations activities requires firm creative guidance from a single source to integrate public relations and special promotions with the balance of the marketing activities. Other members of the public relations agency work at the direction of the company principal, usually with little or no direct contact with the builder-client.

Principal or Partner. This individual, who may have a varied and extensive background in public relations, media relations, advertising, newspaper reporting, and/or communications, is responsible for all client communications and for developing and implementing a strategy, budget, and creative program for public relations and promotions.

Senior Account Executive. The senior account executive works at the direction of the agency principal to coordinate and implement public relations activities.

Account Manager. The account manager oversees the scheduling and production of public relations and promotional materials under supervision of the account executive.

Advertising Agency

Before hiring advertising specialists, you need to understand how agencies are structured and operate. Advertising firms usually assign a team to each account, consisting of several of the following staff members.

Principal or Partner. This individual has extensive experience in marketing and advertising and exercises overall control of creative and administrative functions within the agency and provides final review of strategies, media plans, and creative directions.

Account Executive. Preferably someone with extensive marketing experience, the account executive is responsible for marketing/advertising strategy and acts as builder-agency liaison.

Creative Director. The creative director either directs a staff of writers and artists or develops the concepts for the advertising program and subsequently directs other staff members to execute the work.

Copywriter. A copywriter writes the words in advertising, coordinates the verbal with the visual, and works hand-in-hand with the art director to complete job assignments.

Art Director. The art director uses design skills to (a) develop graphics for the creative concepts, (b) communicate the graphic and creative strategies to copywriters, and (c) produce final layout and design.

Media Buyer. The media buyer plans the strategy for budgeting, placement, and monitoring of broadcast, print, and outdoor advertising. This individual is often responsible for checking media invoices prior to billing the client.

Production Manager. The production manager is responsible for the estimating and—upon client approval—purchasing of all printed materials, including such items as stationery and brochures.

Research Director. In a large, full-service ad agency, the research director manages the in-house research necessary to maximize the effectiveness of the marketing/advertising strategy.

Graphics Designer

Designers determine the design, format, and fabrication materials used in each element of the graphic displays. Assisted by the builder and other members of the marketing team (or by an in-house copywriter), the graphics designer coordinates copy and titles as needed.

Fabrication Staff. These people manufacture or produce the graphic displays and any special installations—for example, display cases or topographical tables—according to design specifications.

Interior Designer. Interior designers determine the floor coverings, wall coverings, stock furniture, and accessories required to furnish reception areas, offices, closing rooms, and other areas in the information center.

Creative Artist or Copywriter. In large agencies these individuals develop logo and image materials, signage designs, marketing brochures, and collateral sales materials.

If you were to select and retain a marketing consultant, a land planner, and an architect—the people who use the results of market research and preliminary site engineering to design the site and homes—you would generally would do so at the beginning of the control phase. Usually builders select any other marketing specialists prior to construction in accordance with the scope and nature of their assigned responsibilities. The bar chart in Figure 3.10 illustrates typical timing for contracting design and marketing specialists for a new community development.

Small-Volume Builders

Many small-volume builders can save money without sacrificing quality by directly retaining experts in each marketing field for which they need professional expertise, rather than hiring large agencies. For example, a builder can retain a sign painter and a writer directly without going through an advertising agency.

FIGURE 3.10 Typical Timing for Contracting Marketing Specialists

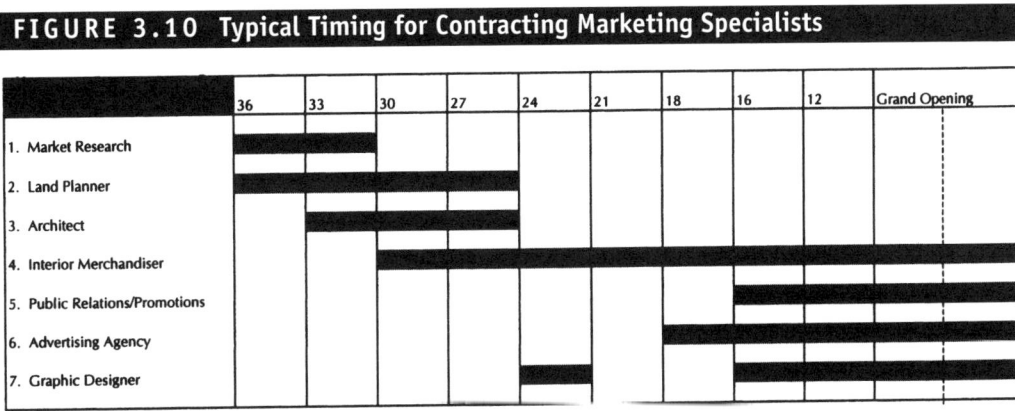

Although this method requires more coordination on the builder's part, the builder can procure high-quality services at a lower cost than to contract with a single firm for a wide variety of services, some of which may not even be required. On the other hand, some small-volume builders may believe that their time is better spent on other aspects of their business and therefore prefer to use a single agency for coordinating all marketing services.

Specialization and Expertise

Overlapping areas of expertise are common among marketing specialists. For example, advertising agencies, public relations agencies, and graphics designers (and sometimes even architects and interior merchandisers) all may offer image creation brochures and sign design and production. Similarly a single firm may claim expertise in public relations, promotions, advertising, signage, and information center design and graphics.

This overlapping expertise is illustrated by the triangles in Figure 3.11. Overlap most frequently occurs in areas of secondary expertise and capability. In those cases in which more than one firm is involved, you should limit contract responsibilities to each firm's primary areas of expertise to assure the highest possible quality of the final marketing presentation.

However, benefits occur when each firm or individual specialist's work is reviewed and critiqued by other marketing team members with strong secondary expertise. Thus, the merchandiser may review architectural plans, an advertising agency may comment on information center displays and signs by the graphic designer, and a public relations specialist may sharpen ad positioning.

Locate Marketing Talent

Finding the best persons for each job is a universal management problem. Because marketing constitutes a tiny portion of the cost of each new home—quite disproportionate to its value in attracting revenues—you should consider retaining only high-quality marketing specialists. The secret to cost-effectiveness is to spend more money on talented people who can devise ways of spending less money on marketing per dollar of revenue.

Where are the talented marketing specialists? You usually need only look carefully in your local market area, and at the competition. Additionally you should see what is working best in your particular market area: in newspaper advertis-

FIGURE 3.11 Marketing Team Selection

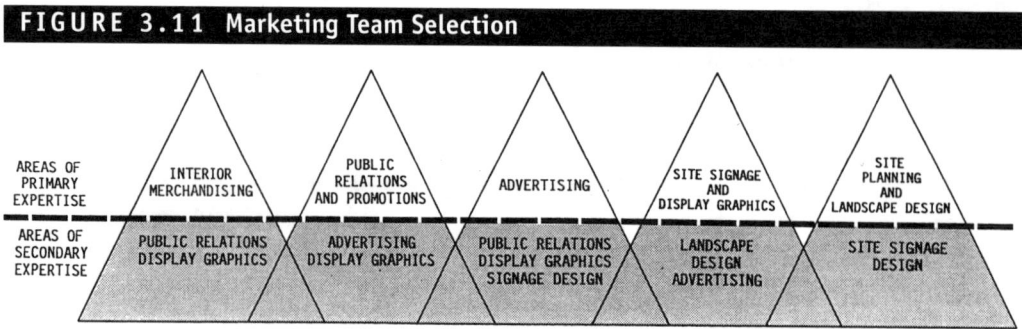

ing, in magazine and newspaper articles about new homes, in new community and builder signs, in displays and brochures, and in model home merchandising—the "What's Working Best" principle. You can then find the specialists who created the best of these marketing elements and (a) retain their companies, (b) hire the creators to moonlight, or (c) hire them to work full-time (depending on builder volume and the person's particular specialty).

Another method of selecting marketing specialists is by identifying local, regional, and national firms with appropriate expertise. The search may begin locally and continue in ever-widening circles until you identify two or three qualified firms or individuals. Obtain recommendations from colleagues and from local and national building associations. You could consider for new work architects, land planners, graphics designers, or marketing consultants who have worked with you in the past. They can also be a source of referrals. Ask newly selected team members for later selections.

The Selection Process

Choosing needed professionals for a marketing program should be an ordered selection process, and you should award work on the basis of comparative qualifications and cost estimates. In some cases this process may result in multiple assignments to a single firm; more often, you will award limited contracts to two or more specialists.

After checking references, ask promising candidates to formally present their work. When more than one candidate is invited to present a proposal, you should provide each with the names of others under consideration. This procedure permits scheduling of consecutive interviews on the same day and apprises candidates that they are in a competitive situation. Marketing professionals should not object to limited competitive situations and will appreciate the professional courtesy of this information. On the other hand, some will reasonably refuse to compete for work if an excessive number are under consideration because preparing and presenting a preliminary proposal is costly.

The Presentation Process

Marketing professionals making presentations for specific work should demonstrate previous work with slides, photographs, or original materials. Conceptual presentations or discussion of marketing strategies for the current project are also appropriate at this point. Such professionals usually do not provide detailed proposals unless you pay a special design fee or retainer.

Before a marketing specialist can prepare a proposal, you must provide adequate background information. Market research results usually are distributed in advance of presentations, including absorption rates, pricing and square footage recommendations, target consumer profiles, and competitive product information. In addition certain specialists will need specific items. For example, the architect will need the land plan, and the interior merchandiser will need the architectural plans.

During the presentation process, you may request interviewing assistance from other members of the marketing team. For example, the architect may be present during interviews of interior merchandisers or land planners. The general marketing consultant also may participate. Having others present can prove expensive, however, so builders should limit such assistance to critical selections or those in aspects of marketing in which they have little experience.

Make the Final Decision

After the specialists have made their presentations, you should lose no time in reaching a decision. The professionals who have invested their time and talent in presentations will appreciate equivalent professionalism from you in the form of a prompt decision. Once you reach a decision, all parties should be informed immediately so that new work can be organized and scheduled properly.

Important concerns in the selection process are balancing the strengths of marketing specialists and creating a team that will work well together. A professional team has no room for prima donnas; individuals selected should have experience in the team approach to problem solving. Figure 3.12 is a general evaluation form that you can adapt for each type of marketing specialist.

Communication Guidelines

Proper communication is essential to effective teamwork. Equally important is a clear understanding of how decisions will be made and communicated.

As discussed earlier, you should schedule—and all marketing specialists should attend—regular marketing coordination meetings. These meetings usually are held monthly but may be more frequent during the critical period immediately prior to the grand opening of a new community or product line. At these meetings each specialist should report on the progress of work and/or current completed work for review, comments, and approval according to a written agenda.

Many builders establish communication guidelines or procedures at the start of a new project. Typically, either a member of the builder's staff or the general marketing consultant is designated as the information coordinator. Circulating information to other marketing specialists is the responsibility of the coordinator.

The following guidelines will ensure effective communications among all members of the marketing team:

- Give each marketing team member a list of the names, firms, street and e-mail addresses, and telephone and fax numbers of all team members.
- Encourage team members to communicate directly with each other to expedite the exchange of technical information and better coordinate problem resolution.
- Send all marketing team members copies of all correspondence, graphics, and printed materials submitted to the builder.
- Require that all graphics be submitted in a standard size for presentation (for example, 24×30 inches).

You also may establish guidelines for decision-making. Usually, approvals for work are communicated through a single member of the builder's development team. This individual also is designated to receive and review all incoming communications from team members for appropriate internal circulation.

FIGURE 3.12 Evaluation Form for Marketing Specialists

I. Capabilities
  1. Size of Staff:_____
  2. Number of years in business: _____
  3. Annual billings:_____
  4. Annual building industry billings:_____
  5. Type of builder experience
     Single family detached: _____
     Attached or multi-family: _____
     Commercial/other: _____
     Luxury priced residential:_____
     Moderate priced residential:_____
     Lower priced residential: _____
  6. Size of typical residential
     Development:
       Acres:_____
       Dwelling units: _____

II. Success Qualifiers

  1. Identify any builders or developments
     on the firm's client list that are known
     for creativity:
     _____
     _____
     _____

  2. List the firm's current clients that are
     Experiencing excellent sales traffic:
     _____
     _____
     _____

  3. Note problem/solution situations
     cited by the firm:
     _____
     _____
     _____

  4. Membership in professional
     Organizations:
     _____
     _____
     _____

  5. Honors/awards:
     _____
     _____
     _____

III. Organization and Compensation
  1. Who will be assigned to your
     account, and what will their
     responsibilities be?

     _____
     _____

  2. Briefly describe the fee structure
     of the firm:

     _____
     _____

**III. Results of Interviews, Reference
      Contacts, and Site Visits**
  1. Note the three things that
     impressed you most favorably
     (a,b,c) and least favorably (x,y,z)
     from the prospectus, or interview:
     a. _____
     b. _____
     c. _____
     x. _____
     y. _____
     z. _____
  2. Note the three most and least
     favorable comments that were
     received through contacts with
     former or current clients:
     a. _____
     b. _____
     c. _____
     x. _____
     y. _____
     z. _____
  3. Note three things that impressed
     you most and least about current
     advertising campaigns that were
     demonstrated to you through
     copies of ads or other graphics:
     a. _____
     b. _____
     c. _____
     x. _____
     y. _____
     z. _____

II

MARKET

Marketing is communicating with consumers to attract them to a product as well as ensuring an outstanding presentation of that product in support of the selling process. It consists of four interrelated components: identity, public relations, advertising, and merchandising. The first three components attract consumers to make a contact (inquiry) with the sales team, either by phone, mail, e-mail, or in person. If the contact is by one of the first three media, you need to use additional communications to attract the consumer to visit the community and thus initiate the selling process. The fourth marketing component, merchandising, supports the selling process through impressing site visitors, either before or after they make an inquiry.

4

Marketing Action

Aprogram of marketing action is an outcome of the strategic marketing plan presented in Chapter 3. It involves establishing and periodically reviewing marketing priorities to ensure efficient coordination of the four market components—identity, public relations, advertising, merchandising—through the all-important launch campaign and thereafter through sellout.

Set Priorities

Ensuring consistent allocation of time, energy, and money to marketing is a continuing concern for builders. Some builders are interested primarily in craftsmanship or financial returns, with marketing relegated to the bottom of their priority lists. Such minimal attention invariably produces minimal results.

The necessary time commitment to marketing management varies according to each builder's personal work habits and efficiency. Overall time commitment also varies in relation to each builder's personal involvement with each of the four market components. For example, a builder easily could devote as much time thinking up a new ad concept as on a new house design. But most builders have neither the time nor the inclination for such time-consuming marketing tasks.

The modern builder is equipped with a computer to help allocate time priorities. You should devote approximately 10 percent of your work time to marketing management (for example, one-half day per week) exclusive of sales, closings, and individual research activities. This time allocation will vary throughout the year, depending on the stage of development and marketing preparation. However, you can achieve exemplary marketing management within this time allocation provided that you organize marketing according to the following guidelines.

Master Action Program

The Master Action Program presented in Chapter 3 defines the sequence of activities from plan to sellout. It illustrates the minimum time commitment for each activity and the overall program, and it is accompanied by program guidelines to describe each activity. A variety of computer software programs can help you schedule the Master Action Program, including off-the-shelf programs advertised in *Builder* magazine and other home builder publications. In addition systems analysts can custom-design programs for individual builder operations.

Sequence

You must carefully control the sequence of marketing activities. For a new development, public relations should be an early priority to publicize the theme and special characteristics of a new development or model home. You want consumers to be somewhat familiar with them when you launch an advertising campaign to attract potential purchasers to the site. You need to defer advertising and merchandising until you have completed your market research, product definition, planning and budgeting, and identity creation. You need to have all aspects of the new home product established before you prepare communications for consumers. If you plan to merchandize a model home, you should retain the interior merchandiser during product definition to critique architectural design from an interior perspective.

Minimum Time Requirements

Minimum time requirements include 2 to 4 weeks for identity creation, with a similar time period following identity creation for concept formation and program definition. Merchandising production normally requires 12 weeks (community and model), and advertising production varies up to 4 weeks depending on the type of ad. Of course, your team can prepare advertising and merchandising in parallel.

Master Action Plan Guidelines

Appendix A illustrates sequence and timing guidelines for a Master Action Plan for a typical new product.

You can produce such guidelines on any computer spreadsheet program, such as Lotus, Quattro Pro, and Excel. For maximum efficiency in allocating front-end expenditures, the builder must determine a realistic date for model home completion and key the entire marketing action plan to this date. Upon completion, the action plan becomes the framework for managing all marketing activities throughout the launch campaign of a new product offering or the annual marketing maintenance program of an ongoing product offering. Each of these cases is addressed on the following pages.

The Launch Campaign

Well before the launch of a marketing campaign for an offering of new homes, you need to identify all relevant marketing tasks with their optimum lead times and allocate responsibility for the various tasks to specific individuals. A model launch campaign organizer appears in Appendix A to help guide you through this complex process.

Launch Campaign Organizer

The sample launch campaign organizer contains over 100 separate tasks relevant to marketing new homes. These tasks extend through all phases of the new homes marketing system to ensure a comprehensive marketing approach. Simply mark out any inapplicable tasks. As with any such list, absolute comprehensiveness is difficult to achieve, particularly given the large number of terms and techniques used in advertising and merchandising. You can readily add new tasks to the launch campaign organizer for unanticipated situations.

Lead Time. Accompanying each launch campaign organizer task is a suggested lead time from the estimated grand opening date. These lead times have proven sufficient in dozens of successful applications and take into account necessary prerequisite and follow-up activities suggested in the third and fourth columns of the launch campaign organizer. The fifth column lists the lead-time date of follow-up activities, thus bracketing completion time for that task. Actual start and finish dates for each task are provided, along with space for the name of the person responsible for successful completion of that task. Even if an agency is involved, a single person should be responsible for each specific task.

Computer Adaptability. The launch campaign organizer is readily adaptable to computer software for network programs such as those applying critical path method (CPM) and performance evaluation review technique (PERT). The launch campaign organizer serves as the input data for the program. Output is usually in the form of a bar chart indicating critical path tasks—those tasks that must be accomplished within assigned times in order to meet the grand opening deadline.

Preparation and Distribution. During implementation of a launch campaign, after you have prepared the launch campaign organizer with responsibilities for particular tasks, you need to present it to each member of the marketing team. Progress updates are reported at regular team meetings throughout the implementation period.

Marketing Maintenance Program

The marketing maintenance organizer presented in Figure 4.1 can guide you and your development team through biweekly review and control of all marketing

FIGURE 4.1 Marketing Maintenance Organizer 1; Bi-Weekly Marketing Checklist

	OK	Problem	Responsibilty
Public Relations			
Publicity Articles			
Newsletters:			
Consumer			
Broker			
Promotions:			
Consumer			
Broker			
Advertising			
Media Placement:			
Newspaper			
Magazine			
Direct Mail			
Radio/Television			
Ad Content			
Community Merchandising			
Overall Condition of:			
Entry Sign			
On-site Signage			
Trailblazers			
Model Identification Signs			
Information Center Sign			
General Community Appearance:			
Entrance			
Landscape			
Model Area			
Entrance and/or Model Flags			
Visitor Parking Area			
Amenity Areas			
General Community			

activities. It provides a checklist of ongoing activities that require regular performance evaluation and possible modification. For example, if a selected newspaper advertisement is not generating sufficient consumer inquiries, you would reevaluate the ad and possibly modify or replace it. Regular review of marketing activities using the marketing maintenance organizer allows you to uncover weaknesses and strengths.

Program Coordination

Successfully managing a marketing program requires coordinating people, tasks, and creative concepts. This coordination is best achieved through regular marketing coordination meetings at least monthly for most campaigns. The launch campaign

FIGURE 4.1 *Continued*

	OK	Problem	Responsibility
Condition of Information Center			
Desks Clear			
Tables Clear			
Carpet Clean			
Exterior Ashtrays Clean (no smoking signs)			
Displays in good condition			
Refreshments Stocked			
Collateral Information Stocked			
Interior Merchandising **Condition of Models**			
Carpet			
Drapes			
Furniture			
Accessories			
Bathrooms			
Beds			
Walls			
Free of odor			
Closets free of debris			
Stolen items?			
Selling Operations Inventory			
Meeting brochures			
Sales brochures			
Inserts			
Move-in kits/gifts			
Purchase agreements			
Stationery			
Warranties			
Other documents			
Owner Relations Referrals			

organizer or marketing maintenance organizer can serve as the agenda for these meetings (Figure 4-2). New community launch campaigns, particularly in the early stages, often require weekly team meetings to ensure efficient coordination.

Marketing Trade-offs

Marketing coordination is relatively easy when it involves exchanging information among team members. Difficulties arise when "What's Working Best" principles—direct reliance on proven strengths—imply potential trade-offs between different functions. For example, a builder may experience a surge of inquiries after publishing an article in the local newspaper, but few inquiries from advertisements placed in the same newspaper. While some advertising agencies will argue long

---

FIGURE 4.2 Typical Agenda: Marketing Coordination Meeting

1. **Dwelling Design**   E. Winters
   - Final approval of working drawings
   - Estimated construction start dates
   - Estimated model home center completion date

2. **Public Relations/Promotions**   N. Drury
   - Pre-opening activities
   - Grand opening schedule/plan of events
   - Approval of final guest list
   - Review of consumer newsletter

3. **Identify Creation**   L. Smith
   - Logo review
   - Stationery Package
   - Brochure

4. **Advertising**   L. Smith
   - Introduction of creative concept
   - Recommended media budget/schedule
   - Pre-opening communications

5. **Merchandising**   B. Dowell
   - Pre-opening signs
   - Entry sign design/installation date
   - Street sign design review
   - Information center design

6. **Action Schedule**   Chairman
   - Public relations
   - Identity
   - Advertising
   - Merchandising

---

and loud about the benefits of image advertising, multiple exposure, and message frequency, the indisputable fact remains that the ads did not generate prospects while the publicity did. Therefore the marketing manager faces a difficult decision: Should he or she shift expenditures from advertising to public relations? If the manager does so and it works, homes will sell more rapidly and everyone (with the possible exception of that advertising agency) will be happy. Clearly a good manager may not please everyone when using "What's Working Best" to achieve marketing cost-effectiveness.

Gordon French of Denton, French, Daniels advertising agency in Tampa, Florida, maintains that experienced new home advertising professionals would not argue against the trade-off described above. On the contrary, Gordon states that modern advertising is based upon solid performance data that result in regular shifts in advertising and public relations allocations. He suggests that a continuing increase in reliance upon performance data will guide consumer communications in the future.

Meeting Coordination

Every team member may not need to attend every marketing coordination meeting. Only insist on the attendance of those directly involved with current issues. Ensure that each team member has a list of all team members with addresses and telephone numbers to encourage regular communication between meetings.

Continuing adherence to a regular schedule of marketing coordination meetings, and relegating all nonemergency marketing and sales issues to such meetings will result in cost-effective marketing. Successful builders control their marketing through planned coordination, rather than allowing marketing decisions to be thrust upon them sporadically.

5

Create
an Identity

Abuilder's overall marketing message must be based upon an
appealing identity or image in all marketing communications.
Logo, name, and image-support materials are the identification symbols by which a building business becomes known. You can create
your business identity with the help of graphics specialists, advertising agencies, or public relations firms—whoever does the best identification logos and accompanying collateral materials in the area.

Logo Design

Company and community logos provide graphic identity and continuity, enhance advertising, and facilitate immediate visual recognition. They are used on business cards, stationery, signs, information
center graphics, brochures and promotional items, and in print and
electronic advertising. Repetitive use helps consumers in your market
develop a visual identity for your firm and community based upon
recognition of the logo.

The key to using a logo is consistency. It should appear in exactly
the same form in all of your consumer communications. Its repetitive
use and importance to your reputation mandate careful design
through adherence to the following guidelines.

Clarity

Consumers do not analyze logos. Logos register an impression on
the eye and in the mind nearly simultaneously. Thus a logo can be

84

considered a form of visual shorthand that should be clean and simple in both typeface and graphic image.

Flexibility

A logo will be reproduced on a variety of materials in many forms, ranging from ads of every size through outdoor signage to promotional name tags. It should remain legible when reproduced in a size small enough for a business card or a Web-site application, yet should be bold and beautiful if used for brochure covers or graphics for the sales office. When designing a logo, the marketing team must consider the multiple uses anticipated and ensure that the final design meets every need.

Distinctiveness. A logo's purpose is easy and immediate identification. If it appears similar to the logo of another builder or business in the area, this advantage is lost. Your logo should be as distinctive and recognizable as your homes.

Colors

You should keep target markets firmly in mind when choosing colors. For example, empty nesters usually prefer muted or more traditional colors such as navy blue and burgundy red over bright, vivid hues. A first-time buyer, on the other hand, is attracted by the vibrancy of primary and secondary colors such as red, yellow, and green. If you are one of the many builders who target more than one market segment, the colors you select should produce a positive reaction in all of the target groups. Like the logo itself, logo colors should be suitable for a variety of marketing applications. The Color Institute in Washington, D.C., can provide more detailed information on the use of color.

An example of a color error is an unnamed builder in a metropolitan market who began business as a custom builder. He created a logo in black and gold that symbolized the sophisticated designs and craftsmanship he produced. However, when he expanded into the starter-home market he was dismayed to learn that potential young consumers considered his company unfriendly and aloof to their interests. The logo colors were not the sole cause of this problem, but they definitely contributed to it.

Cost-Effectiveness

You must keep the overall advertising budget in mind when developing a logo. You do not need to have a four-color logo. In fact, the logo must reproduce well in black-and-white printing. A one- or two-color logo is less costly to reproduce on stationery and sales materials. Similarly embossing and gold- or silver-foil printing may seem attractive initially, but they are costly on business cards or brochure covers.

Logo Examples

Figures 5.1 and 5.2 illustrate examples of logos that are distinctive, easy to read, and reproducible in a variety of materials. Figure 5.1 is a corporate logo and Figure 5.2 is a community logo; both have been well accepted in their markets.

FIGURE 5.1 Corporate Logo

FIGURE 5.1 Corporate Logo

Community and Model Home Names

Appropriate names for a new community and its model homes assist consumers in memory recall and thus help build your image. In addition, evoking an emotional response from a name is far easier than from a number. For example, potential purchasers will relate better to The Hampton than to Plan 2103.

Names should convey an attractive and accurate image. A community developed on meadowland should not be called The Woodlands any more than contemporary designs should be named for historic places. Many builders select a theme for their names based upon actual landmarks: mountains, woods, rivers, or hills. Others choose romantic, historic, or nautical themes. The simple rules in the paragraphs that follow make selecting names for communities or homes an easier process.

Consistency

Once a name is selected, the builder has, in a sense, selected a theme for the balance of the community as well. Conversely, if the community is already named, model names should tie into the established theme. Whether you choose a landmark, topography, history, or wildlife as a theme, consistency reinforces that image.

Simplicity

The name should be easy to remember. A short word or two is easier to incorporate into a logo than longer ones, but avoid unusual foreign words. A marketing specialist may speak fluent French, but most potential purchasers in the United States do

FIGURE 5.2 Community Logo

not. People are uncomfortable with words they have trouble pronouncing. You should do everything possible to avoid making potential homebuyers feel ill at ease.

Individuality

Every community is different from its competition, and that difference should apply right down to its name. Builders should check the real estate section of local newspapers to avoid adopting names others are already using. A good source of inspiration for names are books, magazines, place names, and information relating to the characteristics of the development property.

Figure 5.3 shows two columns of names. To name a community, a name from the first column can be matched with one from the second. For model homes, names should be selected from the first column that are compatible with the community theme. When selecting a community name or logo, the principle of stop, look, and listen can be useful:

- The name should be sufficiently distinctive to cause the person seeing it to *stop* and take note of it.
- It should *look* attractive so that the person seeing it will remember it and what it stands for.
- The name should *listen* well—that is, be pleasant to the ear.

Builders should trust their instincts. If a possible name, spoken aloud, does not sound right to you, it probably will not sound good to a potential purchaser.

Builder Credibility Message

Consumers become purchasers more readily if they believe in your credibility to achieve high-quality performance. Every builder needs a concise message in text and pictures to convey his or her qualifications and experience to consumers. First you must earn an excellent reputation through a history of proven success and then communicate it in believable fashion to potential home buyers. A sample builder credibility message follows:

Over Forty Years of Leadership

WILMAC Corporation, developer of Regent's Glen, was founded in 1957 with a single facility in south central Pennsylvania. Since then, the company has grown to eight senior lifestyle communities in Pennsylvania and Florida, employing over 1,500 workers.

WILMAC is a leader in the full range of adult lifestyle options including retirement living, assisted living, home healthcare, pharmacy services, subacute care, Alzheimer's care, rehabilitation, and long-term care. In Naples, Florida, WILMAC operates a specialty hospital for the treatment of eating disorders and chemical addiction and was a partner in the area's premier residential developments, Quail West.

Still a family-owned and managed business, WILMAC is dedicated to exceeding the expectations of every member of our "family," including residents. As we plan for the needs of senior adults in the 21st century, we look forward to the challenges ahead with confidence and enthusiasm.

FIGURE 5.3 Community and Model Home Names

Column 1		Column 2
Trees	**British Names**	**Places**
Apple	Ascot	Bridge
Beach	Brittany	Brook
Elm	Buckingham	Club
Evergreen	Cambridge	Creek
Hickory	Camden	Crossing
Laurel	Castle	Dale
Maple	Devon	East
Oak	Dorset	Farms
Peach	Epping	Garden
Pecan	Evesham	Glen
Pine	Foxhall	Hill
Redwood	Grasmere	Lake
Spruce	Greystoke	Landing
Timber	Hampton	Lea
Trees	Hampshire	Manor
Walnut	Kings	Mere
Willow	Kingsley	North
	Pembroke	Place
Seasons	Regency	Plaza
Autumn	Regents'	Point
Fall	Royal	Ridge
Spring	Stapleford	Riding
Summer	Stafford	Run
Winter	Summerset	Shire
	Wellington	South
Water	Westminister	Square
Bay	Windsor	Valley
River	Wyndham	Village
Sea	Wynmoor	West
Water		Woods

Marketing and Sales Brochures

Builders require two types of brochures: (a) a marketing brochure of modest size and cost with general builder and product information for distribution to consumers by mail or handout and (b) a sales brochure with enough detailed information about the community and new home designs to reinforce the on-site selling process. You should include your builder credibility information in the sales brochure and summarize it in the marketing brochure.

The marketing brochure is usually folded to rack size (4 × 9 inches) from larger stock, although it can be any convenient mailing size. This brochure provides only limited information because its purpose is to prompt a visit to the site. You do not want to provide so much information that a prospect can reach a decision without a visit to the community. Therefore the marketing brochure does not contain floor plans or price information. Figure 5.4 illustrates the cover of a successful marketing brochure.

Conversely the primary purpose of a sales brochure is to reinforce selling information once the prospective purchaser has visited the site. Appropriately this brochure contains more detail. Today's new home purchasers typically visit a home several times before making a purchase decision. At the same time these purchasers also visit other new home communities. Consumers who are retired average even more visits than primary home consumers prior to a home before purchasing it. However strong the initial impression, your homes must remain in the consumer's

FIGURE 5.4 Marketing Brochure Cover

mind and eye for as long as that prospect takes to make a decision. Your brochures are an essential marketing tool for reinforcing this impression.

Brochure Guidelines

The guidelines discussed in the following paragraphs will help in brochure development:

Consistency. Brochure copy and artwork should be consistent with the other advertising and marketing materials. Maintain continuity so that the prospective buyer clearly remembers what is being sold.

Brevity. Brochure copy should be complete, concise, and provide all the information a consumer needs. A wordy brochure is rarely fully read, although retirees demand more detail than young consumers.

Color and Paper Selection. Printing in four color continues to be more economical each year and should be compared with a one-or two-color production with respect to cost. However, even one color of ink on colored paper can prove attractive and effective in conveying both image and message. Select your paper stock with great care and make sure the quality is appropriate to the product identity. Even for modestly priced products, the paper should be heavy enough to feel substantial; yet it needs to be light enough to fold cleanly.

Flexibility. The information in a brochure typically changes over time as you add new models, alter elevations, or change standard features and finishes. For this reason many sales brochures consist of a cover with an inside pocket fold (Figure 5.5). The cover frequently uses the builder's logo as artwork and is printed in the company or community colors. The back cover of the brochure may contain copy or information that does not change—a community locator map or builder credibility message, for example. The balance of the information usually is printed on insert sheets placed in the inside pockets to allow for inexpensive updates.

Price Information. One item you should not print in the brochure itself is a price list. Prices change frequently and should only be quoted by the builder or a sales associate. Before giving the brochure to a prospect, the price of the preferred model should be noted on the corresponding floor plan or elevation. Writing this price in green ink (a distinctive, nonaggressive color) with a date is a subtle urgency close, implying a limit to the time that the home can be purchased at the price quoted.

Brochure Contents. A typical sales brochure should contain the following information:

- logo
- builder credibility message (listing builder qualifications and history of accomplishments)
- community story and lifestyle information
- elevations (often only those of interest to specific prospect receiving brochure)

FIGURE 5.5 Marketing Brochure with Inside Pocket Fold

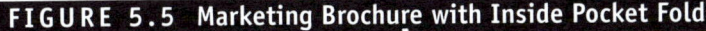

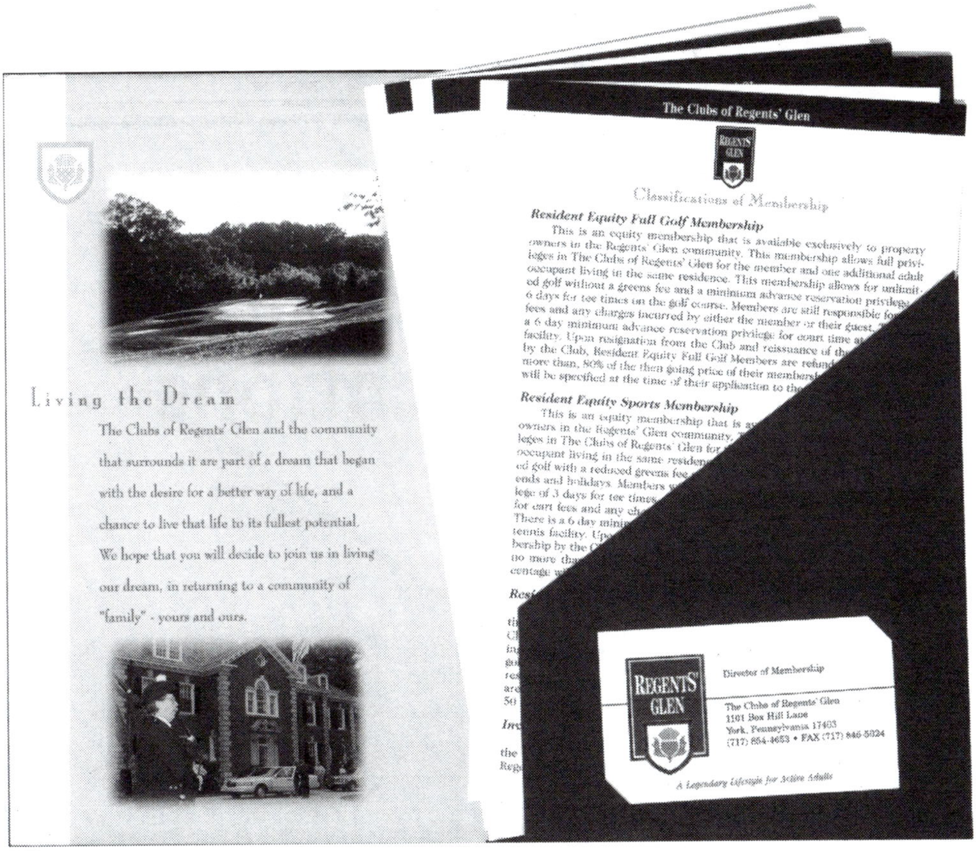

- floor plans (often only those of interest to specific prospect receiving brochure)
- features and benefits (luxury appointments, construction quality, specialty items)
- area map
- site plan
  - street and e-mail addresses, telephone and fax numbers
  - option list (optional)
  - financing fact sheet (optional)
  - space or holder for a business card (optional)

You would supply the information for each of these pieces, which are prepared by a professional advertising, public relations, or graphics agency. The agency usually submits each item to you for approval as well as the entire package prior to final production.

6

Profit from Public Relations and Promotions

Anew home is the single most expensive product most Americans purchase. Because it is expected to increase in value through use, it serves the dual purpose of providing shelter and being a major investment. Therefore consumers are justly concerned about how well a home is made and the reputation of the persons who produce it. You can address many of these hopes and fears about a new home purchase directly through public relations.

What Is Public Relations?

Public relations is the art of inducing the public to have understanding and goodwill about a person, organization, or product. It is image building through community commitment and sincerity. For you as a builder, it encompasses all contacts between your business and the general public. Its purpose is to improve your image and enhance your identity through explicit or implicit third-person credibility. Public relations operates on the principle that what other people say about you and your business may prove more believable than what you or your advertising agency states.

The implied third-party endorsement of skillfully produced publicity can be your most cost-effective traffic generator. Media publicity in newspapers, magazines, television, and radio attracts consumers' attention more effectively than paid advertisements. In addition face-to-face contacts arranged through promotional events provide strong opportunities for impressing individuals with your confidence and sincerity.

This chapter describes methods for planning a public relations campaign and the individual components of the campaign. It also includes both on-site and off-site promotions as well as the elements of community relations.

Plan a Public Relations Campaign

Whether undertaken in-house or by a public relations agency, a public relations campaign should always incorporate the following five steps which are subjected to the performance evaluation described in Chapter 9:

- identify the target audience(s)
- assess current image
- define objectives
- generate program components and preliminary schedule
- estimate expenditure budget
- refine program in harmony with overall marketing plan and budget

Target Audience
The target audience (prospective new home purchasers) is generally defined through market research. Public relations also seeks to influence community and government leaders as well as potential homebuyers. However, a PR campaign may incorporate specific elements directed at only a portion of the overall target consumer group. For example, a development aimed at first-time purchasers may contain a combination second or third bedroom/study designed expressly for couples who need a separate work space at home—a feature that can be publicized specifically to this segment of the target consumer group. Other elements of the PR program may be aimed at other segments, with some elements designed for the all of the targeted groups.

Current Image
You need to assess your current image needs with respect to the opinions of your target audience. Surveys and focus groups described in Chapter 1 are the best means of conducting this assessment.

Objectives
Public relations objectives include image building that establishes credibility in the community. Thus public relations supports overall marketing plan objectives (sales absorption and consumer inquiries), as well as more detailed objectives for particular segments of the program. PR objectives that support various marketing programs should be in writing, along with alternative program components, scheduling guidelines, and costs.

Program Components
The public relations objectives can be achieved economically by carefully coordinating PR components. You should strive for a cost-effective balance on expenditures for publicity, newsletters, promotions, and in some cases, community

relations. For example, you can usually combine article writing and photography for the four elements listed above.

Coordinating the various components of the PR program requires a schedule defining the priorities and relationships of program elements. Each element must be undertaken as soon as necessary input is available.

Expenditure Budget

Each of the PR elements listed above cost money whether they are completed by in-house staff or outside consultants. These costs must be estimated in advance for inclusion as a separate public relations line item in the overall marketing budget. Because public relations provides a consistent on-going message, it requires consistent funds.

Marketing Themes

The final step in planning a PR campaign is to refine the components described above, with respect to both subject matter and timing, in harmony with other components of the overall program. Marketing themes must be expressed consistently in advertising, public relations, promotions, and merchandising. This refinement requires the efforts of the full team at marketing coordination meetings. However, you can speed up the coordination process by circulating preliminary and final programs to team members for critique prior to decision meetings.

Generating new ideas for a PR campaign usually requires intense creative brainstorming. Such brainstorming frequently gives birth to key themes for marketing new products. You should be prepared to modify advertising and merchandising programs accordingly. Figure 6.1 illustrates a PR program for a home builder, indicating relationships to advertising, merchandising, and sales programs. The theme is enjoying the environment.

Elements of a Public Relations Campaign

Publicity

The most common form of public relations is publicity in print and broadcast media; you can generate publicity through news releases, awareness mailings, and newsletters. Newspaper, magazine, and broadcast publicity has the advantage of exposure to a large audience, but it has the disadvantage of lack of control over content, timing, and frequency of messages. Therefore many builders control their publicity. They target a selective audience through newsletters, news releases, and awareness mailings.

Real estate public relations consultant Mike Wilson of Atlanta points out more than half of print and broadcast news is not generated by staff reporters, but rather comes from someone outside the media acting as a publicist. When such publicists meet the writing standards of media editors, they become credible news sources with continuing media relationships. Whereas news reporting does not distinguish between positive or negative impact on subjects, the publicist, according to Wilson, is focused on accenting the positive and overcoming the negative on behalf of a specific client. Thus, the successful publicist combines writing skills

FIGURE 6.1 Themed Public Relations Program

Stage	Public Relations	Advertising	Merchandising
1. Site plan	■ Concept publicity; Including announcement of renowned naturalist on development team ■ Promotional events presenting master plan to (1) VIPs and (2) neighbors near the site	■ Plan/Campaign ■ Photography by nature specialist ■ Ad Production	■ Plan/information center ■ Displays/signs production ■ Model's interior design
2. Construction	■ Groundbreaking publicity re-emphasizing preservation ■ Promotional event presenting plan and products to real estate agents ■ Broker newsletter recording above event	■ Image ads featuring "Live With Nature—by Design"	■ Construct information center ■ Construct entrance ■ Install information center ■ Install models ■ Install on-site directional signs
3. Sales	■ Preparation of special purpose brochure on birds and other environmental features ■ Grand Opening of information center and models preceded by broker preview and press/VIP event ■ Consumer newsletter recording Grand Opening and announcing nature programs ■ Implementation of public nature programs on weekends directed by naturalist ■ Publicity on nature programs	■ Call to action ads featuring residents enjoying natural environment ■ Directional billboards ■ Direct mail program to target consumers	■ Entrance, perimeter fence and signage compatible with natural environment in environmental setting enhanced with display photos of residents enjoying nature ■ Information center complete ■ Merchandised model homes overlooking environmental feature (exterior colors selected to blend with nature) ■ Sales brochure features environmental photography
4. Occupancy	■ Publicity on first resident and continuing community activities ■ Quarterly real estate agent newsletter emphasizing successful cooperative agents ■ Semi-annual consumer newsletter emphasizing residents' enjoyment of environment ■ Periodic broker competitions with awards (e.g. vacation trips, dinners, cash) for participation and sales ■ Periodic site events for residents and guests to generate referral sales	■ Success ads featuring residents enjoying community amenities including nature observation tower	■ Street signage

with access to the editors of major media. Although builders can generate publicity in both print and broadcast media, these resources are more consistently exploited with the assistance of a professional publicist with established contacts and credibility. However, with or without a professional publicist, you should befriend and seek to understand news media people. If you provide them with accurate newsworthy releases, answer their questions promptly and efficiently, they may seek you out for comments on other homebuilding-related matters.

Print Media. This type of publicity varies for newspapers and magazines. The former require fresh news in a concise format, and coverage will likely take up less space but have more immediate news value than magazine publicity. Magazine articles can be longer, with more detail and more photos than newspaper coverage. However, magazines require materials at least 2 months in advance of publication. Weekly newspapers provide a compromise between magazines and daily newspapers on publicity length and detail. In addition, weeklies usually have small staffs that are eager for articles, thus providing a more receptive vehicle for builder articles.

Feature articles are written to appeal to a broad audience of readers—often in a conversational style. They may include interviews or third-party endorsements. The following list is of possible topics for feature articles:*

- Community profiles
- Architect interviews
- Natural or man-made amenities
- Third-party endorsements by satisfied homeowners
- Housing trends
- Customer preference surveys
- Best-selling models and why
- Consumer education on homeownership

You can establish credibility by publishing consumer-related articles, but don't try to sell houses with these articles. News is defined as something out of the ordinary, and you need to make sure your press releases are newsworthy articles. Focus on what is different and why it is important to the homeowner.

In addition, you can cash in on publicity by having prepared a brief description of the best benefits and features and a sketch of the exterior for each new home and by fostering and cementing relationships with local newspaper and magazine writers.

You should express your enthusiasm for your new homes when socializing with writers. Builders can often meet writers at builder association events (Parades of Homes, for example) or can invite writers to meet them over lunch or at a new home opening.

Broadcast Media. Broadcast media need a constant flow of news and news updates. "Hard" news coverage requires human interest stories of unusual impact rarely available to builders, but weekends are generally slow news days and may provide publicity opportunities. Broadcast news requires that the marketing team think in terms of the ear rather than the eye (as in print media), with brief, active, and easy-to-understand copy.

---

*Adapted from *Home Builders Publicity Manual: A Step-by-Step Guide for Successful Public Relations* by Deborah Johnson (Washington, D.C.: National Association of Home Builders, 1984), now out of print.

The two best publicity opportunities for builders in broadcast media are public service announcements (PSAs) and special feature programs. Although a building company cannot advertise under the guise of PSAs, many opportunities exist for capitalizing on them, such as sponsoring a seminar or hosting a community event at a building site. Figure 6.2 provides a PSA example. Route all PSAs to each station's public affairs director.

Special feature programs, programs devoted to specific topics of interest to the community, are more difficult to penetrate unless you are a key official of a builder association or similar organization. However, real estate developments with unique features and appeal have attracted broadcast media.

Press Kits

These kits are compilations of news releases, fact sheets, photos, and other pertinent information about specific communities that can increase opportunities for media coverage of a new community or a distinctive model home. All the information is packaged in a folder with pockets for materials, preferably with community identification printed on the front. The printed folder often can be used at later stages of development to distribute other information. The following paragraphs provide details about the many elements of an effective press kit.

News Releases. News or press releases are the main ingredient of any press kit. They must be prepared in correct form and error-free. Most busy editors and reporters welcome well-written, concise news releases. A journalistic rule-of-thumb when preparing news releases is to answer the Five Ws:

- Who is involved?
- What happened?
- When did (will) it happen?
- Where did (will) it happen?
- Why and how did (will) it happen?

The lead paragraph of a news release should concisely state the most important fact and following sentences should be of decreasing interest. Thus, when the editor cuts for length, the key points will remain.

The following two lists provide further information on the news release format:

FIGURE 6.2 Sample Public Service Announcement (PSA)

The annual Junior Diabetes Benefit Festival will be held on Saturday, June 12th, from 10 AM to 4 PM at the Seven Oaks Community Center. The 5K run gets underway at 10 and the children's games start at noon. Of course, the petting zoo and refreshment booths will be open all day. Festival Chairman Jim Jones of the Seven Oaks Community staff reports that they are expecting a big turnout again this year, so come early and bring the entire family for a fun-filled day. Phone Jim at 555-1000 for more information.

Note: PSAs for broadcast media must be concise to fit a 15-second, or occasionally a 30-second spot. They must not

- Release date—Lists the date after which the release may be published.
- Builder—Names the builder about whom the release is written. Use builder's letterhead.
- Contact—The name of the person to contact for further information. Both office and home telephone numbers are given since some editors write on weekends or in the evening.
- Subject—Suggests possible press headline and tells what the story is about.
- Lead—The lead establishes the theme of the story. The first few paragraphs should reveal the pertinent information—the Five Ws.
- Page continuation—The word *more* at the foot of all but the last page in a release denotes additional copy in the event the pages become unstapled.
- Page identification—Each page should be identified by builder, slug line (story subject), and page number.
- End of release—The symbol ### or 30 at the end of the release tells the editors where the story ends.
- Editor's note—Asks editors to verify with builder timely information contained in the story that occasionally is subject to change. The editor's note should also include the name and telephone numbers of the appropriate person to contact.

Tips for writing releases—

- Type double-spaced on one side only of $8^{1}/_{2} \times 11$-inch paper. Do not use carbons or odd-sized paper.
- Use upper and lower case letters.
- Do not underline words for emphasis.
- Leave 1-inch margins on each side of the page and at least 2-inch margins at the top and bottom of the page for easy editing.
- Do not break paragraphs between pages.
- Always address releases to specific editors.
- Keep releases short, about two or three pages.
- Always date releases at the top of the page and type in all capitals the words *FOR IMMEDIATE RELEASE* or provide a release date.
- Make sure releases have complete and accurate information.
- Use simple, direct language. Do not try to be clever or folksy. Opinions belong in the editorial pages, so do not fill releases with hype or fluffy adjectives.
- Spell names correctly. Always include two initials or the full first name of an individual and his or her title for the first reference. Use last name only for subsequent references.
- Double-check for typing, grammatical, and spelling errors.
- Send a cover letter with each release if possible.
- Stories should have a local angle that specifically relates to the community in which the target publication is distributed.
- Become familiar with and meet newspaper deadlines.
- Hand deliver the release whenever possible.

A typical news release format is illustrated in Figure 6.3. In addition to this two- or three-page format, you can virtually ensure your name in the local busi-

FIGURE 6.3 Sample News Release Format

public relations inc.

press release

Contact:
Mary Kay McCune
Mike Wilson Public Relations, INC.
404/365-9000

MORRISON HOMES CHOSEN AS BUILDER
IN CELEBRATION, FLA.

For Immediate Release

ATLANTA – (October 1997) – Morrison Home, Inc., America's fastest growing national homebuilder, has been chosen as one of the homebuilders in the master planned community of Celebration, Fla.

Morrison Homes was selected after an extensive application process that included a financial review, in-depth interviews and surveys of Morrison Homes homeowners.

"While we met the stringent criteria for home building in Celebration on paper, what set us apart was our consistent track record of quality building and customer service," said Steve Parker, president of the Orlando division of Morrison Homes. "We provided the names of more than 600 of our homebuyers to The Celebration Company for a customer satisfaction survey. What they found was that our customers were overwhelmingly satisfied with the work we did and would recommend our company to a friend or family member."

Courtesy of Mike Wilson Public Relations, Inc., Real Estate Public Relations Consultant, Atlanta, Georgia.

---

ness news on a regular basis by submitting one- or two-sentence announcements of awards, promotions, special events, and similar news to the business editor.

Fact Sheets. Another integral component of press kits, fact sheets briefly list all pertinent facts about the subject in concise and readable fashion. They provide reporters background information on which to base an interview or write a brief news item. A fact sheet should contain the following:

- Development concept (if applicable)
- Opening date(s)
- Location
- Size of homes (often includes room measurements)
- Design team
- Special benefits and features
- Community amenities
- Builder story
- Builder employee story
- Other particulars

Feature Articles and Photography. Interesting, well-researched feature articles can be useful additions to press kits, particularly when they are accompanied by professional photographs and computer disks.

For most publicity, photography should consist of clear, professional black-and-white glossy prints sized 5 × 7 or 8 × 10 inches. (Many magazines increasingly require color transparencies.) Editors prefer photos that incorporate unusual subject matter and human interest scenes. Photo captions, also called cutlines, and should be brief, complete, and include left-to-right identification of people. The number of people in a photograph should be limited to three (and never more than five). Check with the newspaper for appropriate caption format.

Although advertising photography for magazines is largely in color, photography for newspaper publicity—and for that matter, newspaper advertising—is generally black-and-white. Publicity photos usually are informal, while ad photos are carefully posed. Thus, photos must be taken separately for each of these purposes. If you use a single photographer for both purposes, you may save money).

Dealing with the Media

Media people face constant deadlines and time pressures as standard parts of their jobs. Some enjoy the pressure; others react adversely to those around them during tight deadlines. Respect their deadlines, call them when you say you will call, and provide them with concise, honest answers without unnecessary embellishment.

Newsletters

A newsletter is a cost-effective controlled-publicity tool that provides information to a select audience with implied third-person credibility. While the reader may understand that you sponsor the newsletter, the format, design, and article content can imply third-person credibility if they are executed properly.

Clearly, newsletters are best produced by professionals, but they normally can be generated quickly, relatively inexpensively, and in several formats for different audiences. Because of their production speed and cost, newsletters often become the marketing program's most important informational tool. With newsletters, you can distribute new, interesting information rapidly.

Newsletters are intended to supplement, rather than replace, marketing brochures. They serve as follow-up mailings to prospects and owners, as well as handouts to update development progress. Most builders should distribute two types of newsletters: a full-color (or, if budget demands, two-color) consumer newsletter and a one- or two-color newsletter for real estate professionals. Although the former piece also may be sent to real estate agents, the latter is designed expressly to appeal to their business interests. It often is a single page printed on both sides and folded in thirds. A third type of newsletter, for internal corporate communications, is common in large organizations.

With the emergence of more sophisticated personal computer software (such as Pagemaker and Corel), most offices have the technical capability to produce newsletters in-house ready for printing. Thus, the issue for many builders is whether a staff person has sufficient aptitude and time to produce a newsletter. If not, a professional is required.

Consumer Newsletters. This type of newsletter (Figure 6.4) is usually distributed to all prospects and owners quarterly or semi-annually, depending on the scale and type of development. Consumer newsletters are preferably in full color for full consumer impact. An effective newsletter can be four $8^1/_2 \times 11$-inch panels (printed on both sides of an 11×17-inch sheet of good quality paper). A newsweekly format for text, such as that used in *Time* or *Newsweek*, often works well. The newsletter should contain brief articles of interest to homeowners and potential owners, such as a feature article on a homeowner, a description of a community amenity or special feature, a profile of a key staff member, and benefits of new product features. The consumer newsletter should also contain photographs (again, in color if possible) of people enjoying themselves in their homes. You should avoid boring exterior elevation photos or drawings of homes.

Newsletters for Real Estate Agents. These newsletters (Figure 6.5) should be the same size and format as the consumer newsletter. They are distributed to selected, high-potential real estate agents and brokers who may generate prospects for a particular home or development—not just to broker's offices. These newsletters contain special articles of interest for real estate professionals, such as your policies and procedures for selling homes and a picture and story of an agent who recently received a full commission selling one of your homes. This newsletter can be a one-color, two-panel job (both sides of a single sheet), but it should be distributed more often than the consumer newsletter (at least every 3 months) to ensure the real estate community's continued interest.

Awareness Mailings. Just as newsletters are mailed to selected prospects or real estate agent lists, awareness mailings of publicity article reprints, special announcements, and promotional event invitations can go to these same people. Therefore establishing and maintaining prospect and agent mailing lists is a crucial part of the public relations program.

Promotions

Builders sometimes confuse promotions with parties held to entertain friends or subcontractors. Rather than being purely social events, promotions are serious efforts to generate face-to-face interaction between you (and/or your salespersons) and your new home prospects, real estate agents, and influential members of the surrounding community.

If carefully planned, promotions should be the most cost-effective component of the marketing plan. Both on-site and off-site, they have proven to be effective generators of new prospects and motivators for undecided prospects and real estate agents.

FIGURE 6.4 Consumer Newsletter

SPECIAL HISTORICAL ISSUE

The Front Porch

Volume 1 Number 1   The Community Newsletter of Lakewood Ranch   1996–1997

The Traditions of Yesterday, The Hometown of Tomorrow

For nearly a century, the land of the Schroeder-Manatee Ranch has been used as a working ranch. Raising cattle. Growing trees and grasses. Producing fruit and vegetables. Now, the same care used to run a successful ranch is applied to its latest addition: a new hometown.

Lakewood Ranch has been designed using the best ideas from both the past and the present to create a hometown of tomorrow. Half the land has been set aside for open spaces and recreation areas to maintain the natural beauty of the ranch and to create new areas where residents can gather and enjoy life. The balance of the land has been divided into five unique villages offering places to live for everyone. Rounding out the plan will be commercial areas to provide residents with convenient services and employment opportunities. An extensive infrastructure of roads, sidewalks and trails will connect all areas of Lakewood Ranch together to provide for convenient vehicular and pedestrian travel.

Each village will have its own special lifestyle and appeal, attracting many new residents. Like hometowns of the past, the villages will be made up of small neighborhoods. Each neighborhood will feature a variety of home styles in similar price ranges to maintain the highest property values for all residents.

Wherever possible, Lakewood Ranch will incorporate the best and latest technology. Non-potable water for community irrigation, natural gas, underground utilities and fiber optic communications systems are just some of the innovations planned to make Lakewood Ranch the hometown of tomorrow – today.

More than anything, Lakewood Ranch will be a community designed to feel like home to all its residents for years and years to come. There's a lot to like about having a hometown around the house. We invite you to put Lakewood Ranch around a new home of your own. ◆

Lakewood Ranch is a place for families of all ages.

A Master-Planned Community

Master-planned, like so many catch-all phrases, is one that crops up often in the community development industry. Many communities claim to be master-planned. However, few can actually deliver. Lakewood Ranch is the area's only true comprehensive master-planned community.

According to urban planners, a genuine master-planned community is one that combines all the components of urban life.

In essence, much like a small hometown, a master-planned community is one that provides opportunities for homes, services, employment and recreation for all segments of its population under a comprehensive plan for responsible, environmentally friendly growth.

The visionaries at Schroeder-Manatee Ranch first embraced the concept of a true master-planned community many years ago as they saw an opportunity to bring forth Florida's newest "hometown" under a comprehensive plan. One that embraced both the needs of people, nature and the environment.

Over ten years of planning have set the stage for Lakewood Ranch. Places

The master plan provides for man, nature and the environment they share.

to live, work, learn, play, shop and worship will all be a part of the community. And, to ensure that the promise of the plan will be a continuing reality, representational governing bodies, in the form of Community Development Districts and Home Owner Associations have been established.

We invite you to learn more about Lakewood Ranch and discover the *Nature of Florida Living* the way it was meant to be – truly master-planned for today and tomorrow. ◆

Places to live will be enhanced by places to work and play at Lakewood Ranch. Above, the Summerfield Community Park is a popular place for resident events and gatherings.

Inside This Issue

2 Ranch R&R
   A Place To Learn

3 Meet The Builders

4 Commercial Opportunities
   Community Sponsors
   Add Value to Life

FOLDOUT Site Plan Poster

FIGURE 6.5   Real Estate Agent Newsletter

Reflections

LIVE WITH NATURE · BY DESIGN

David F. Parker of Clark Parker Associates shows brokers the house plans at The Sanctuary.

Watson agent kicks off broker sales with a client from Pennsylvania

The Sanctuary name has become known even as far away as Pennsylvania, and an agent from Watson Realty Corp. has made the first outside REALTOR sale to a client from the Keystone State.

Helene S. Edwards, a realtor-associate and broker-sales associate who has spent all of her nine years in the business with Watson, said that the Pennsylvania client was specifically interested in a nature-oriented community. She was shown a number of properties around town — the Arlington and Mandarin areas as well as the Beaches — and when she saw The Sanctuary she was sold on its beauty and ambience.

Helene S. Edwards

Ms. Edwards said the client brought down a friend from Boston, and she was so impressed by The Sanctuary that her family is trying to transfer here just so they can buy a home at the community.

The client, according to Ms. Edwards, specifically liked the planned nature trails and the nature watch tower.

REALTORS to preview models at The Sanctuary

Area REALTORS will preview the newly-opened Sanctuary models at a special broker party Wednesday, February 15, from 4 to 6 p.m.

The Sanctuary is now selling at **pre-construction prices** until the Grand Opening to the public, which will be held on the weekend of March 11.

The Sanctuary has commissioned an original painting by local wildlife artist Lynne Fascetti Mayhew that will be used as the cover of the invitation.

If those receiving an invitation will bring it with them, Ms. Mayhew will sign the invitations as a limited print. These are the only prints that will be made. At the end of the event there will be a drawing, and someone will receive the signed original. This is Ms. Mayhew's second limited edition release.

REALTORS attending the event will view the new model center, tour the three furnished models and be given an overview of the community.

The Sanctuary offers 3% commission

The Sanctuary is "cooperating" — in a big way. The community is offering a cooperative REALTOR commission of three percent through its on-site agents from Baita Realty Inc. The commission will be paid upon closing of any transaction at The Sanctuary with a client registered at the on-site information center.

Professionals from any recognized REALTOR may register a client by personally accompanying the client to the information center for a sales presentation. After obtaining qualifying information from the client, a marketing representative of The Sanctuary will conduct the sales presentation, including a tour of the information center and the models.

Since on-site sales persons sell only The Sanctuary, and their compensation is the same for cooperative REALTOR sales, each will give their best effort to assist you in closing your sale.

Registration protects the REALTOR for 60 days, subject to double registration procedures.

On-Site Promotions

This type of promotion depends upon the target group and specific objectives. For example, special promotional events such as a grand opening or national neighborhood day may generate new prospects, particularly if you advertise for this purpose. To generate media publicity, these events may feature a magic show for children, hot-air balloon rides for young couples, or an on-site interior designer for empty nesters. You can sponsor move-in parties that include a new owner's friends to generate referrals. Low-cost promotional events include a children's petting zoo (using animals from a local zoo), a builder-sponsored long-distance run for participants of all ages, or a fly-casting contest in a water feature (using a rubber-tube target).

Many builders extend personal invitations to real estate agents to join them for coffee and Danish during caravan days—the specified days on which all agents in an office tour new listings as a group. Such promotional events with personal contact are likely to generate higher cooperation in future years as competitive production builders get larger and more impersonal.

Off-Site Promotions

These promotions most often are associated with trade show and shopping center displays used by large-volume builders and resort developers. However, small-volume builders with upscale products often succeed with informal, off-site presentations held in the homes or clubs of existing owners or friends of owners. Service and social clubs also provide opportunities for off-site presentations. Such presentations must be made by trained representatives supported by a concise (approximately 8 minutes) audiovisual presentation and/or displays presenting the benefits and features in a low-key manner. Such promotions often are initiated by asking homeowners or friends to invite a few selected guests who might be interested in your homes, and you handle all reception arrangements and expenses.

Community Relations

Community relations include interactive volunteer events as well as individual participation in community and professional charitable organizations within the market area. These types of activities establish commitment to your community and help you gain the respect of community and government officials, They provide forums for maintaining relationships with government officials and lenders as well as providing publicity opportunities to promote credibility through the methods described earlier in this chapter. These relationships will become even more important in the future as development sites become more scarce and government regulations become more stringent.

Most of these community relations require no professional support, but some activities require strong coordination to organize and publicize your company's team of volunteers, for example, special volunteer programs such as Habitat for Humanity's homebuilding program for the financially disadvantaged and special community projects such as building a children's playground. Maxine McBride of Clockwork Marketing in Sarasota, Florida, maintains that participation in these kinds of community volunteer programs can generate long-term positive credibility if it is systematically planned from the initial decision to participate. She provides assistance to builders by coordinating such activities. For example, she arranges for team hats and shirts and publicity articles with pictures during the preparatory stage as well as during the event itself. Volunteer activities provide a strong supplement to community relations, and when properly designed and carried out, they can generate referral prospects for your new homes.

You also may experience challenging situations requiring professional community relations assistance. Detecting these potential problems prior to their emergence will prove cost-effective. The following paragraphs discuss four common situations that may require the design and implementation of a community relations campaign.

Zoning and Subdivision Approval

Current residents in a community may react negatively to the development of neighboring properties. Such reactions—usually normal concerns over disturbing the neighborhood status quo—often can be neutralized through personalized presentation of the facts. However, with sudden and often unexpected press and political support, the concerns of a few neighbors can escalate rapidly into a major obstacle to government approval. As you initially plan the development, you must recognize this potential problem, which has stymied many well-intentioned development plans. To avoid such a problem, planning the development also needs to involve organizing a detailed community relations campaign of information distribution, promotional events, and publicity releases to generate positive support from neighbors, government officials, and the press.

Homeowner Associations

These associations often organize in opposition to the builder/developers that gave them birth. Issues may include controling association activities and budget, maintaining and operating of recreation and landscape amenities, and transfering of ownership of such amenities to the association. Even the most personable and well-intentioned builder can be transformed into a villain almost overnight, with disastrous publicity marring his or her reputation in the greater community. Such problems can be foreseen and prevented through a community relations campaign directed at owners and the press.

This example demonstrates the value of having a good image and reputation. Community involvement and education consistently done will help cement builders as caring about their communities and help them garner public support when it is needed. In such situations stress the positives, don't be defensive, tell the truth, and position yourself as on the right side of the issue.

For example, a clear concise statement describing community association responsibilities and outlining the transfer of control from builder to residents should be provided in your promotional material as well as in your formal association documents. Repeatedly clarifying potentially disruptive issues in community newsletters will help prevent misunderstandings and unnecessary resident-builder conflict. As another example, some builders effectively reduce customer service call-backs through regular newsletter columns on household maintenance.

Litigation and Arbitration

These two distinct and often unpleasant situations are unfortunately common for many builders. If you are faced with litigation, you should enlist the services of a community relations specialist at the same time you hire an attorney to establish means of protecting your builder's image during the ensuing unpleasantness. Because private arbitration occurs outside the courts and may indeed be self-imposed, a community relations expert may not be necessary.

Additionally, community relations campaigns often are directed at the litigation or arbitration participants themselves, as well as at the press, in an effort to achieve settlement outside the courts whenever possible. Sometimes, the campaign is devoted to minimizing public information—a task often requiring as much professional guidance as the effective dissemination of information.

Loan Applications

In addition to the preceding situations, many builders find it useful to enlist community relations expertise for assistance in presenting major development loan applications to financial institution executives. Appealing presentation and packaging often make the difference between acceptance or rejection.

7

Advertise for Results

New homes advertising must generate the steady flow of new home consumer inquiries critical to reaching your sales objectives. For example, if you historically convert 5 percent of inquiries to sales (conversion ratio) and advertising generates 40 inquiries per month, you should budget for 24 home sales annually ($40 \times 12 \times .05$). If you wish to increase sales, you will need to undertake a more aggressive advertising program to increase the number of consumer inquiries.

This chapter examines present and emerging forms of advertising for new homes. The objective is to increase your knowledge of these communications to achieve more cost-effective results.

The Need for Advertising

Advertising is the means of telling prospective new home purchasers about your product through paid sales messages. It differs from public relations in that you can define your message and present it with precision not possible in a publicity article. Advertising aids a builder and/or community development in the following ways:

- targets the appropriate consumers
- distinguishes the builder from the competition
- establishes a distinctive identity or image
- communicates specific product information
- maintains real estate agent awareness of products

Builders use print advertising, outdoor signs, direct mail, radio, television, and the Internet to market new homes. Each of these types of advertising is examined on the following pages.

Multiple Languages and Cultures

The United States is home to people from many backgrounds. First- and second-generation immigrants from other countries customarily still prefer their native language and retain cultural symbols and preferences that may differ substantially from each other.

People of Latin and Asian heritage are the fastest growing minorities in this country; those from Spanish-speaking backgrounds will soon become the largest minority. African-Americans are taking increasing pride in their cultural and linguistic history along with dozens of other smaller and equally proud minorities. English words and symbols do not provide appealing communications to many of these groups. More importantly, some words and symbols actually have negative reactions from persons of other cultures. Therefore, in examining the following guidelines for advertising, keep in mind that you must review all messages—both verbal and graphic—for impact on various cultures.

If target consumer groups contain substantial numbers of one or more minorities, you should seek expert advice from specialists in communicating with these groups. Over future years, sensitivity to diverse cultures will become increasingly important to successful advertising.

Print Advertising

Most builders who are expanding their businesses rely upon newspapers as their primary advertising medium to attract the attention of potential purchasers and motivate them to call or visit the new homes site. Magazines are a second form of print useful to these builders. Following are guidelines to different types of print ads, their design, and technical application.

Buyer Motivation

An advertisement's graphics and headline should draw readers into the ad and make them want to read further. Simply attracting their attention, however, is not enough. A successful ad also must motivate the reader to action—either a telephone call or a visit to the site. In other words, good ads deliver prospect inquiries and qualified traffic. To accomplish this objective, ads must offer the reader a benefit. The benefit can be real (such as cost savings) or perceived (such as move-up lifestyle, convenience, or comfort). Both types of benefits are important because new home builders sell not only a home, but a dream of a new life.

Advertising executive Toni Alexander of Intercommunications in Newport Beach, California, believes that we may need to reexamine a trend toward lifestyle images to attract consumers:

> In the 1980s, most builders got bored showing the product so they shifted to lifestyle images. Over the years, these images became bromidic and did not reflect the lifestyles—

much less the needs and values of today's buyers. So, maybe it's time to go back to the old days and focus on the product and make it different, not just the advertising.

Some builders already have been advertising new product ideas that are attracting purchasers. Morrison Homes marketing specialist Diane Morrison, now in Austin, Texas, combined talents with architect Doug Sharp of Bloodgood, Sharp Buster, in Des Moines, Iowa, to develop Imagination Space—expansion of the hallway connecting children's bedrooms to accommodate toy storage, personal computer, study alcove, or other elements used by more than one child. Builders in Florida are adding a room behind the family room called Opportunity Space, which purchasers are using for such functions as office, hobby room, and music room. And Atlanta builders have enjoyed considerable success promoting a Bonus Room in attic space above the garage or in some cases future expansion space in the third bay of a three car-garage can accommodate a children's playroom, live-in help, grandparents, or older children returning to the nest.

Types of Newspaper Advertising

Newspaper advertising consists of classified ads and display ads. Both are effective in certain circumstances and should be considered carefully when buying newspaper space. Both types of advertising may be a cost-effective way to reach potential homebuyers. Therefore most builders should allot a substantial percentage of their advertising budget to newspaper advertising. The newspaper real estate section is the first place prospective homebuyers and area real estate agents look to see what is available.

Classified Ads

Classified ads are usually all print, with no artwork, illustrations, or photographs to set them apart—with perhaps the exception of a small logo or special border treatment. Classified ads usually run only in specified sections of the newspaper and are smaller than most display ads.

Classifieds: Why and When. Classifieds ads are an economical form of advertising for builders of all sizes. Because classified ads are the primary source of private home sales outside of realty firms, many prospective home consumers turn to classifieds first. Therefore you should use classified advertising continuously. If you alternate slightly different messages every week you will avoid presenting the same message constantly.

Buzz Words. The use of buzz words attracts the reader's attention in classified advertising. Sample buzz words include the following:

- privacy
- builder financing
- built to last
- custom-made
- great schools
- hot tub
- friendly neighbors

Dos and Don'ts of Classified Advertising. The following suggestions will help you avoid common mistakes when planning classified ads:

- Do use a boldface line above or at the start of an ad.
- Do use a special border treatment to stand out among other ads.
- Do not use "call for appointment."
- Do not run an ad of over five lines.

Display Ads

Display ads run throughout a newspaper and can be up to a full page or more in size. They usually contain artwork or photography. Graphic ads found in the real estate section of a local newspaper are display ads. You need not place a large ad to draw attention to your homes, but you must create a position that is different from other builders in the area. Figures 7.1 and Figure 7.2 show successful display ads. These ads also are suitable for local real estate guides or other black-and-white publications distributed in a particular local market.

Buying Newspaper Space. Assuming that your ad agency does not buy your newspaper space, you can purchase it yourself economically (although not as economically as a large advertiser such as an advertising agency or real estate broker). First, obtain the newspaper's rate card listing all information needed to place an ad. The rate card provides demographic and circulation figures, as well as size, type, and deadline specifications. It also outlines advertising costs and discounts for multiple insertions during a specific time period. You may then select the schedule of advertisements appropriate to your budget to determine the price per column inch per insertion. Note that a contract for an insertion schedule obligates you to a higher rate if you fail to meet the schedule. Some publications are more likely to provide publicity space to advertisers.

Artwork. An intriguing photo or illustration can catch the consumer's eye at a glance. If competitors are showing elevations, lifestyle artwork will set an ad apart. Similarly, if many current newspaper ads use white type on a black background, you should avoid this technique. The key to being noticed is being different, yet on target. Mere imitation is often self-defeating.

Headlines. A clever, punchy headline can entice, provoke, and draw attention to an ad. If it contains a consumer benefit, so much the better. However, headlines should not try to tell the whole story; they should simply lead the reader into the body copy and illustrations. For example, "1999 Builder of the Year" or "Award-Winning Builder" might entice a reader to continue reading.

Shape. The shape of an ad should also be different from the competition. If several others are running one-quarter-page vertical ads, a one-quarter page horizontal ad may bring good results.

White Space. Because the most effective ads tell a simple story, usually filling an ad with facts and figures is a mistake. White space—vacant space without type or artwork—is "smart space," it makes the ad easier to read and giving it an attractive appearance.

FIGURE 7.1   Ad for Retirees Parallels Family-Oriented Ad

Before Eagle Harbor's amenities were completed, the advertising featured a young girl coming down a waterslide to convey a message of fun and excitement in a new family-oriented community. With the introduction of low-maintenance patio homes for the retiree market, this new ad featured an actual resident shot on site. It mimics the original one and presents a two-fold message: The community is still the perfect place to raise children and also a great place for an active retirement.

Courtesy of East West Partners of Florida, Orange Park, Florida; ad agency, Morgan and Partners.

A Prominent Element. A single element in every ad should be most prominent. A simple test involves turning an ad upside—down to see what stands out. The headline? The logo? An illustration? If everything blends together and competes for attention, the ad's overall impact will be diminished. Potential buyers must notice an ad before they can read it, and they must read it before they can act on the information in the ad.

FIGURE 7.2 Your Dream Home

BUT A DREAM

That's what life is—when you row your boat.

Every schoolchild knows it's true. Which is why your new home

should come with a lake. A big lake. And plenty of rowboats.

And a spa and tennis courts and parks and

long, meandering hiking trails.

And great blue herons nesting in old cottonwoods

on something called an isthmus.

Hey, it's your dream.

Might as well make it a really good one.

GRANT RANCH

THE
LAST GREAT
PLACE

Just east of Wadsworth on Bowles Avenue. For more information call 303-295-3808

D.R. Horton	Genesee Company	Larsen Homes, Ltd.	Metropolitan Homes	Richmond Homes	Watt Homes	Semi-Custom Homes	Custom Homes
Single-family homes	*Detached patio homes*	*Detached patio homes*	*Townhomes*	*Single-family homes*	*Single-family homes*	upper $300s to upper $400s	upper $400s to the $800s and above
upper $100s to upper $200s	upper $100s to mid $200s	mid $200s	mid to upper $100s	upper $100s to low $200s	mid $100s	773-3399	
799-0034	*Single-family homes*	792-2252, ext 122	*Detached patio homes*	797-0746	649-9386		773-3399
	upper $200s to low $300s		upper $100s to low $200s				
	526-9000		877-3799				

This preconstruction ad implies that Grant Ranch has everything a potential home buyer might dream of, and the photograph provides a dreamlike quality. "But a Dream" supported the introduction of Grant Ranch as The Last Great Place—an in-fill property, surrounded by well-established, highly desirable neighborhoods on land once owned by Colorado's first governor.

Courtesy of Simeon Residential Properties, Denver, Colorado; ad agency, Miles Advertising, David Miles

What to Include in an Ad. The salesperson's formula of presenting features, advantages, and benefits also applies to advertising. Two mistakes are common in builders' display advertising: too much information and too little information. Ads should strike a delicate balance with certain information included in every ad:

- name of the community and/or builder
- type of housing
- price or price range (luxury housing may be an exception)
- address or direction to the sales location
- telephone number
- information center and model hours
- unique selling proposition (elevation, features, lifestyle, special incentive, special financing, or other buyer benefits)
- builder awards and affiliations (for example, member in the National Association of Home Builders)

In addition to this basic information, every ad should contain a call to action. For example—

- Visit our designer showcase model home.
- Buy today at yesterday's prices.
- Select the best homesite today.
- Visit today to place your name on our priority list.
- Visit today for special preconstruction prices.
- Select a home today for completion before the holidays.
- Special financing available this weekend only.
- Buy today and save $5,000.

NEW FLOORPLANS

Whenever possible, the builder should create an event. You can announce an events by placing a banner or "snipe" across the top or bottom of an existing ad (an attention-getting technique). For example—

- Grand opening, Phase (Phase II, etc.)
- Model homes now open.
- Introducing the all-new "Hampton" model.

These events are changeable supplements to a more permanent advertisement. They lose their affect through repeated use.

Mistakes to Avoid. To place a newspaper ad and receive few or no inquiries is disappointing. When this situation occurs, it is often the result of an advertising mistake that can be avoided by careful planning.

Insulting the Target Consumer. Beware of ads that are sexist, imply racial or ethnic slurs, or talk down to the consumer.

Misunderstanding the Target Consumer. Value-sensitive consumers (described in Know Your Customers in Chapter 1 as "Believers" and "Fulfilleds") rarely respond to status-emphasis ads, and status-sensitive consumers ("Strivers" and "Achievers") rarely respond to value emphasis ads.

"Turn-Off" Words. Technical words and construction jargon do not create an emotional appeal and therefore have no place in advertising. *Homesites* sell better than lots or parcels. *Furnished model homes* sell better than houses. *Owner's privacy suites* sell better than a master bedroom and bath. *Energy efficient* (benefit) sells better than R-30 (feature).

Tedious Detail. Selectively choose the benefits and features to be highlighted in the ad. Quality carpet padding or numerous exterior electrical outlets may be important to a builder, but they are not important to consumers at this point in the sale. With emotional appeal firmly in mind, builders should emphasize items that save time and money or provide convenience and comfort.

Bad Timing. If the weather forecaster is predicting a blizzard or other severe weather, you should cancel all ads that will appear during the storm and immediately afterward. In addition, builders should make sure their ads do not compete for attention with major sporting events, community celebrations, or national or religious holidays so that potential buyers can devote reasonable time and attention to the ads.

Newspaper Supplement

Larger builders and community developers frequently sponsor special supplements inserted in newspapers, particularly in weekend editions likely to attract new home consumers. News articles and photographs of new home products and personalities are organized with advertisements by related sub-contractors and suppliers. Providing you can motivate your related businesses to advertise in such a supplement, the overall cost may be relatively modest. You also can purchase extra copies for use as handouts and direct mail pieces. The newspaper supplement can prove to be a cost-effective form of advertising to generate high volumes of visitor traffic to model openings and other special events.

Magazine Advertising

When considering a magazine ad, you must first define the audience to be reached through a particular magazine and then decide if the overall marketing budget is sufficient to reach that audience cost-effectively through this medium (as compared to direct mail and/or special-section newspaper advertising). Full-color magazine ads created by experienced artists are usually very attractive and appealing to a builder, who may indeed lose sight of objectives in the "bright lights" of a glossy, glamorous image. Some regional magazines sell the front cover and publicity articles along with advertisements. You may want to investigate the cost of advertising in state and local publications for a variety of professions or in regional editions of national professional journals such as medical and law journals. Advertising in new home guides produces leads that turn into sales for some builders. Rates for these guides may be less expensive than magazines depending on use of colored inks and other factors.

If analysis warrants magazine exposure, then most of the criteria set down previously for newspaper advertising are applicable to this medium as well. Article reprints are addressed under public relations in Chapter 6.

Technical Considerations for Print Advertising

When planning for print advertising in a competitive marketplace, you must consider design, production, and printing details concurrent with all creative decisions. Failure to do so can lead to disappointing ads in print. The following paragraphs examine items to consider.

Print Quality. Newspapers are remarkably inconsistent in reproduction quality. Quality varies not only from newspaper to newspaper, but in a single newspaper from day to day. When you have any doubt about reproduction quality, you should use illustrations rather than photographs.

Use of Floor Plans. In general you should assume that consumers will not respond to floor plans as strongly as a lifestyle graphic. They are best used later in a selling situation. In addition, fine lines on floor plans often disappear in newsprint.

Borders. In most cases, a border is an excellent way to separate your ad from those surrounding it. Borders also reproduce well and visually define the ad space.

Typeface. Type comes in a wide variety of styles. A good rule is to keep the type simple and readable. Avoid typefaces that are ornate or involve scrolls or art elements. Ornate type is difficult to read, particularly in small type sizes. In addition, type styles may be boldface or italic—often alternated with standard (Roman) type to add emphasis to headlines.

Type Size. Type also comes in a full range of sizes. The size(s) selected depends upon the overall size of the ad, whether the copy is a headline or body copy, and the amount of emphasis desired. Most newspapers print articles in 8-point type; any type smaller than that will be difficult to read. For body copy, many advertisers select a slightly larger type, either 10 or 12 point.

Typesetting. Although the term *typesetting* is still commonly used, photographic reproduction has replaced the traditional manual process of organizing lead type. Whereas type and style choices formerly were limited by the type inventory of a newspaper or typesetting shop, today you have a wide range of choices available in your desk computer for laser printing and subsequent film production for printing. Anyone with a modern office computer and laser printer can produce camera-ready advertisements.

Truth in Lending Act. Passed by Congress in 1968, the Truth in Lending Act specifies guidelines that real estate advertising, including financial information, comply with mortgage credit terms. Strong penalties for noncompliance mandate that builders review the manual available from the Federal Trade Commission.

Fair Housing Act. The United States Department of Housing and Urban Development (HUD) is responsible for ensuring builder adherence to this legislation designed to prohibit discrimination in the housing industry. All marketing materials and selling practices must be conform.

Every builder should display fair housing posters and signs as well as include fair housing logos in print advertising and brochures. Any suggestion of discrimination by age (except for seniors housing permitted for persons age 55 and older), religion, ethnic origin, sex, or household type is subject to substantial fines under this act. A good reference book on compliance to this law is provided by *Fair Housing Compliance Guide* by Rhonda Daniels referenced in the Selected Bibliography of this book.

State Laws. The laws affecting marketing materials vary throughout the country. For example, some states require builders to list their contractor license numbers in their advertisements. Make sure you understand and comply with applicable state laws as well as federal laws. Ignorance is not an accepted defense.

Outdoor Signs

Many builders consider signs to be their most cost-effective form of advertising. They report 40 to 60 percent of their inquiries are generated from the following sources:

- billboards (not as cost effective as the following signs)
- trailblazers (also known as bootleg or bandit signs because many municipalities rule them illegal on roadsides)
- off-site directional signs (legally located on private property)
- entry signs
- on-site directional signs

In the future, as local sign ordinances become more restrictive, builders will require more innovative forms of outdoor advertising such as the boards on the backs and sides of buses and taxis, inside supermarkets, shopping malls, transportation terminals, bus stop benches, and shelters for bus and train passengers.

In all cases, signs must say something about your homes without being excessively detailed. Concise messages will register or be read more easily than detailed sales messages. You need to remember that most signs are read from automobiles traveling at highway speeds.

The design of the signs should complement the desired community image. Hand-lettered signs present an unprofessional, cheap impression and should be avoided in all cases, including value-priced communities. Signage should help establish the community image through use of the logo and community colors. At times, you also can use signage materials to reinforce that image. For example, natural stone available on the site can be designed into a community entry sign or monument, or Victorian-style homes can feature ornate signs of compatible design.

Billboards

Billboards (including paint boards, electronic boards, and poster boards) play an important role in advertising. They reach many people at a variable cost depending on local and state limitations and customs. Billboards are most effective when used to direct visitors to the site and to reinforce the advertising campaign theme. You can reduce creative costs for billboards by using the company and/or community logo or other existing artwork. This repetition has the added benefit of reinforcing other advertising messages.

Builders wishing to use billboards in their advertising programs should use the following simple guidelines to improve their effectiveness.

When to Use Billboards. Billboards are most effective when used to direct consumers to the property. If such signage is not feasible because of availability or high cost, advertising dollars might better be spent in another medium. Unless an advertising budget is unusually large, image creation through billboards is prohibitively expensive.

Types of Billboards. Builders traditionally have used three types of multipurpose billboards: poster boards (12 × 25 feet), rotary boards (14 × 18 feet) and paint boards (up to 48 feet long). Poster boards were originally so named because the advertising message appeared on paper that could be "posted" at regular intervals. Rotary boards, on the other hand, had their messages painted on vertical panels that could be moved or rotated to frames in various locations. However, today poster boards are commonly painted, and in some locations, paper may be used on rotary-sized boards.

In recent years electronic outdoor signs have become increasingly common, often with three or more different faces rotating at a single location. You can expect to see more sign locations converted to multiface electronic signs in the future.

Each type of billboard is best for particular needs. For example, a builder seeking to establish a logo with a one-time showing would find a poster board on paper most cost-effective. A long-term directional billboard, however, is best suited to a painted rotary board. When choosing between painted or poster signs, builders using only one or two locations should have the message painted.

Location and Position. Billboard costs are based upon scarcity (government limitations) and the amount of traffic traveling on the road on which the board is located—plus the addition of lights to attract traffic 24 hours per day. In other words the number of impressions a board generates determines the relative monthly cost for the location. When investing in billboard advertising you should have at least one board on a nearby major thoroughfare. Before contracting for a specific location, you should drive past and judge each location. A desirable board is positioned so that drivers have an unobstructed view and an opportunity to act upon the directional message.

Minimal Copy. The key to an effective billboard is simplicity—in copy, artwork, and colors. Messages must be brief and easily read; the optimum number of words on a billboard is seven. For example, copy might be limited to the name of the community or builder, price-qualifier ("From the $120,000s"), a telephone number, and a direction ("Straight Ahead 1 Mile").

Bright Colors. Bright, bold colors attract attention to billboards. Many studies have examined which colors are most easily seen from a distance. While red was once considered the strongest, most easily recognized color, many brilliant new paints are available today in striking colors or florescent shades that make any message "pop" off the board. Your billboard colors should maintain continuity with community colors to increase recognition. If a builder wishes to use bright colors that are not in harmony with the community image, a band of vivid color might appear at the top or bottom, carrying directions or a short message reversed out in white or another color.

Lighting. Another factor builders must consider when planning for billboards is lighting to provide maximum exposure on heavily traveled routes. The small premium charged for billboard lighting has proven cost-effective because lighting ensures that billboards will remain readable at night.

Cost-Effectiveness. Many builders save money by leasing land near their sites and constructing their own boards, subject to local sign ordinances. When this solution is not possible, a longer lease on an existing board may be cost-effective. Leases for commercial billboards or poster board locations usually run a minimum of 30 days. The longer the contract, the lower the monthly rate. An outdoor sign company will often agree to repaint a board once or twice a year at no additional charge. Alternatively some builders prepare a special message banner (such as "New Models") to apply to existing billboards and attract fresh interest from viewers at lower cost than a new application of paint.

Off-Site Directional Signs

Trailblazers, bandits and other off-site directional signs are a cost-effective form of outdoor advertising. These small signs are usually preprinted and placed on frames or stakes along roadways to announce a builder's presence and provide directional arrows to a site. Some municipalities restrict the use of trailblazer signs. When permitted, however, they are highly effective in directing inquiries and establishing identity.

Figure 7.3 shows a distinctive trailblazer sign shape that permits the directional arrow to be placed for straight, right, or left directions. To achieve the maximum impact with trailblazer signs, the use the guidelines in the following paragraphs.

Simple Message. Trailblazer signs have only one purpose—to make sure prospects can find the building site. Price or other selling information should not appear on these small signs. Each should contain only a company or community logo and a directional arrow (when applicable), although some builders add the words Model Homes or Models in cases where the logo is relatively compact.

Effective Colors. Trailblazer signs can easily become invisible in a sea of competing signs. Signs with an earth-tone background also tend to blend into surrounding landscape. Try bright colors that harmonize with community or company colors, or a border of bright color can enhance the impact of the central image.

Unique Shape. A trailblazer sign with a unique shape will be quickly recognizable at highway speeds even when the driver misses the logo and name. You might also attach balloons or flags to attract consumer attention.

FIGURE 7.3 Trailblazer Sign

New Off-Site Sign Opportunities

Innovative sign opportunities are being created in most markets. The most dramatic are those on outside of public transportation vehicles providing constantly moving billboards, both for event and image advertising. Signs in transportation terminals (train, bus, trolley, air) and other high-traffic locations are available in both stationary and rotary modes, and painted signs as well. Airplane banners are not new, but they are increasingly used above major sporting events and other crowd situations in a short message format. Other possibilities include bus stop benches and shelters as well as signs at sporting activities including sponsorship of golf holes both on a permanent and individual tournament basis. You must evaluate each of these sign opportunities individually for cost-effectiveness in your market.

On-Site Signs

On-site signs, including community entry, directional, and identification, are discussed in Chapter 8, Merchandising New Homes.

Direct Mail

Direct mail is print, videotape, and CD-Rom advertising that reaches consumers by mail or hard delivery. Its use has increased in concert with increasing information about individuals has become available through the past two decades. Niche marketing is replacing mass marketing. Niche marketing targets identifiable groups of consumers with similar characteristics. Thus, as described in Chapter 1, it targets consumers of varying degree of specificity (for example, you can identify prospects by age, income, wealth, household size, occupation, memberships, purchases, hobbies in terms of a precise location) and communicates with them by mail. You can mail them letters, postcards, flyers, brochures, booklets, pictures, and videos designed to induce action responses.

For example, you can market new home products to targeted first-time purchasers by mailing a special-offering flyer to nearby rental apartments. Management rules at most apartment buildings forbid unsolicited deliveries. If you can get permission to knock on apartment doors, you can have them hand delivered by a service organization and publicize your donation to the organization. A distinctly different example is provided by a Sunbelt retirement community mailing to target consumers in northern states including a video of life in that community with an invitation to a low-price 2-day visit to the community.

Direct Mail Guidelines

Every mailing should have a well-defined purpose and a carefully selected audience. The guidelines in the following paragraphs are specific to direct mail.

Purpose. A direct mail piece can take many forms. The three most common ones are a product announcement, a marketing brochure about the builder and/or product, or an invitation to a promotional event.

Call to Action. Each direct mail piece should contain a call to action or should provoke a specific response. When you are announcing a new model floor plan, you should invite the recipient to visit the new home "this weekend." If you are announcing a price increase, urge prospects buy immediately before the new price become effective.

Direct Mail Follow-Up. Prospect follow-up often involves special mailing pieces. In this case, you should personalize the envelope with a handwritten address and a special-issue stamp, rather than metered postage. Experience confirms that personalized follow-up is more effective than standard printed communications.

Repetition. Use of direct mail, like any other form of advertising, needs to be consistent not used randomly. Just as newspaper ads run several times for optimal results, the response rate to direct mail improves substantially when you send multiple mailings to a target group.

Targeting Direct Mail

A cost-effective response rate from any direct mail campaign depends largely upon careful planning and execution. While the typical response rate to a direct mailing is 1 or 2 percent, this percentage can increase to 3 percent or higher if you repeat the mailing. Response rates are higher for personalized mailings and for invitations to an event. A few tips in the paragraphs that follow can help ensure the best possible cost/benefit ratio from direct mail.

Targeted Mailings. Carefully targeted direct-mail recipients make efficient use of advertising dollars. For example, you can effectively target first-time buyer prospects through mailings to apartment dwellers within a 5-mile radius of the new home location. You can mail to residents in neighborhoods identified with targeted consumers census tract or zip code. Other mailings can be highly selective; a community with an investor program may specifically target accountants. In another location might attract a high number of corporate transferees. Real estate agents are logical targets.

Purchasing Mailing Lists. Professional direct mail companies provide lists based on multiple qualifying factors, such as age, income, and current residence. You must know the market well before contacting a mailing house. The better-defined the target market—both demographically and geographically—the more cost-effective the mailings. Most mailing lists are priced according to the number of names and other characteristics. Lists that include telephone numbers for an additional charge allow personalized follow-up contact after a mailing.

Developing Mailing Lists. For example, visitors to model homes can be recorded and mailed a targeted follow-up. You can even use the Yellow Pages(or a reverse directory (street address listings available in public library) or professional directory if a target market is well defined in terms of profession or current residence location. Reverse directories are available in public libraries and now (for a fee) from some telephone companies, such as Bell Atlantic in the Washington, D.C., area.

Direct Mail Budgeting and Preparation. When budgeting for a direct mail piece, you must include the following costs:

- Cost of preparing the piece, including staff time, design, typesetting, artwork, printing, and binding.
- Cost of envelope, or other packaging for a video tape or printed information on the builder, developer, and new home products.
- Cost of addressing, stuffing, sealing, sorting, and delivering to the post office.
- First- or third-class postage.

A final cost consideration is who will handle your mailings: in-house staff, temporary workers, or a mailing house? This decision significantly affects the final cost and should depend upon the size and purpose of the mailing.

Radio and Television Advertising

These electronic advertising media were considered too expensive for most home builders prior to the 1990s. With the advent of cable television and specialized local channels for community events and real estate advertising, lower cost options became available for television advertising, and radio advertising also became more competitive. Lower production costs for audio- and videotapes and CD-Roms helped decrease overall costs for this type of advertising. However, all of these media still require the expertise and expense of specialists for professional production and effective presentation.

Cost-effective Applications

Builders can best use radio and television advertising to supplement other advertising media to increase traffic at special promotional events, such as model home openings and community festivals. The target audience of the stations or channels selected is all important. Because radio appeals only to the sense of hearing, creative advertising specialists are even more essential. If an agency did a great job generating traffic for a competitor's opening, that same agency could probably produce radio and television advertising for any builder with similar impact.

Two-way communications on television now introduce a whole new era of advertising techniques, and the proliferation of channels continue to encourage competitive costs reductions to make this medium even more attractive in the future.

Reach a Decision

The emergence of closed-circuit television for airplanes, trains, terminals, malls, and the like is an untested medium for most builders that requires further evaluation. Similarly advances in multiple listing services for real estate agents (such as regional listings and rapid response changes) offer additional untested potential.

You should make the decision to include television and/or radio advertising in the marketing plan for a particular product or community during the planning and budgeting stage of the development. Certainly you should consult advertising specialists in reaching such decisions, but the final choice should not rely upon glib presentations or ad hoc additions to a budget made under the pressure of a short-term need. When carefully applied to the need of reaching particular target audiences for particular kinds of products or special events, television and radio advertising are effective media that should not be overlooked. Including an offer for a brochure helps to capture the viewers or listeners for future contacts.

World Wide Web/Internet

The entire communications industry continues making advances in communications through the World Wide Web and Internet. The information highway is attracting new users at an explosive pace and is becoming a more common means of communication. How and when builders should use this medium is the focus of this section.

What Is the Internet?

The Internet is a series of computer networks linked together to form a giant international network of computers that facilitates the World Wide Web (WWW) of communications. Thus, while the Internet is much more than the WWW, it is the connection system that makes the WWW technology possible.

The Internet is connected through telephone lines, and users must have a computer with a modem that can be linked to an Internet service provider (ISP) for a monthly or annual fee. Internet users must have electronic mail (e-mail) addresses to identify them for the purpose of transmitting e-mail and for their Internet connection, and a browser to process WWW information. Internet directories such as Yahoo and search engines such as Web Crawler, Lycos, and InfoSeek are accessed to locate specific information sites. Hundreds of search engines are available. When establishing a Web site, the provider must register a domain name. To establish an information file (or page) on a Web site, the provider must record a unique address using the domain name called a uniform resource locator (URL) that can be identified by online directories and search engines. Consequently, in order to advertise on the Web, you must select a service provider with a Web site who will create your page and place it on the Web for a monthly fee. Alternately, for a much higher cost, you can establish your own Web site.

Advertising on the Internet

According to computer systems and Internet consultant David W. B. Parker of Jacksonville, Florida, "a Web site is like a marketing brochure with interaction." A potential Web-site user must be attracted first by the identification name and then by the prospect of interesting information. Current Internet statistics indicate users tend to have a short attention span, therefore your site must be designed to maintain their interest. You can also provide a quick link to a form that users can fill out to request additional information on a special offering or something else of immediate interest. Supplement this call with a quick e-mail button for users to send messages directly to the site mailbox.

Of course, like all advertising, each page on your Web site must be attractive and contain concise information with appeal for new home consumers. Products targeted to different types of consumers should have individual pages to ensure distinctive messages for their interests.

Since most users access the Web at relatively slow computer speeds, the initial page on a Web site should contain limited graphics that can be processed quickly. Subsequent pages can contain more graphics for display after the user has become interested in the site. Keep it simple is a guideline as important to Web site design as it is to designing outdoor signs. Clearly identify the purpose of the site or page, identify the target audience, plan the design to be attractive and informative as well as including a call to action, and determine who will be responsible for maintaining it to keep information current and record user frequency.

Budgeting Internet Advertising

Establishing and maintaining a presence on the Internet is relatively inexpensive in comparison with other forms of advertising. The ITS design and update costs for a multi-page Web site depends on the established quality and related fees of the designer. But total costs are unlikely to match continuing exposure in newspapers, magazines, or billboards.

As in all forms of advertising, the issue of how much to budget on this rapidly expanding communications medium depends on results from actual use. Effectiveness must be evaluated by the number of consumer inquiries, visitors, and qualified prospects generated from this source; cost-effectiveness, measured by the cost of each visitor from this source, can be compared with other advertising sources to determine budget priorities. However, it appears likely that Internet advertising will be a significant component of your marketing plan in years ahead.

8

Merchandising
New Homes

Merchandising presents actual homes to prospective buyers. Although large-volume builders have presented full-scale products off-site (for example, in exhibition halls or, in at least one case, on the roof of a department store), merchandising generally is confined to on-site presentations. It begins with the community image from the approach road and continues through the high-impact community entry to interior road images and amenities, the information center displays, and finally, model home exteriors and interiors.

The Great Merchandising Debate

New homes merchandising is a controversial subject with many builders, particularly those who cater to modest-income purchasers. The issue is whether a plain wrapper for budget-conscious consumers is more persuasive than the emotional appeal of a fully furnished model. Some builders who cater to value-sensitive consumers maintain that elaborate merchandising negatively impacts these consumers. They may believe that the builder spends too much money on marketing thereby adding to the price of the new home. According to these builders, the budget-conscious purchaser is more likely to be attracted to a competitively priced home in a plain wrapper than to one with a fancy presentation.

Conversely, successful merchandisers argue that expert presentation provides a magnetic emotional attraction to even the most budget-conscious prospect. Merchandisers claim that while the plain wrapper theory is more appealing to the small-volume builder struggling with cash flow allocations, the plain-wrapper advocate usually learns that his or her sales absorption is significantly below the well-merchandised competition. Although most prospects insist upon good value, they are influenced by home presentations expertly tailored to the price range being offered.

The best merchandising for a particular new home offering is distinctive to each local market. The percentage-of-dollar-volume or cost-per-square-foot formulas suggested by some merchandisers are not applicable to all situations. Whatever works best in your market is the appropriate guideline to merchandising. Tailoring merchandising to perceived local consumer demand and competitive product supply ensures the best application of each merchandising element: site signs, community landscaping and amenities, visitor information center, and model homes. Of course, you must balance the total cost of merchandising with other marketing costs in the overall marketing budget described in Chapter 3.

Site Signs

On-site signs consist of the following:

- a community or entry sign/monument
- directional signage to the builderŌs sales location
- identification signage for the information center and model homes
- hours of operation for information center and model homes (possibly with a container for marketing brochures when the center closed)
- thank you for visiting sign on exit route
- construction office directional sign to separate subcontractor traffic

Site Sign Guidelines

For a consistent look, all on-site signs should be similar in design and materials and should feature the community or company logo and colors. Figure 8.1 illustrates a program of typical on-site signs.

Entry Sign. The entry sign to a community makes a statement about the product. It is a key part of the first image for every visitor. Every detail is important, including lettering, fabrication materials, placement, lighting, and surrounding landscaping. The entry sign often is a prospective purchaser's first impression of a builder's quality. Therefore this impression should be positive and lasting.

On-Site Directional Signage. These signs are placed inside the community to direct visitors to model homes, indicate what is being built, and to attract prospective purchasers to inspect it more closely. Directional directional signage may include flags or banners in addition to signs. Even if the model homes and information center are immediately adjacent to the community entry, you should provide a directional sign. These signs and others should be carefully located and maintained for optimum positive impact on all visitors.

FIGURE 8.1 On-Site Signs

Community Entrance Sign

Permanent Model Sign

Permanent Directional Sign

Identification Signs. Signs should inform visitors about guest parking, special amenities, the information center, and the model home area. Many builders place a sign in front of the entry to each model that to identify the model by name. This practice is helpful for attracting consumers in uncontrolled model centers or for visitor identification and recall in high- traffic situations. However, for optimum sales potential, you should ensure that prospects are personally escorted through models.

All site signs convey both image and information. You should ensure that the image is attractive and the information is concise. You also should inspect every site sign at least weekly to replace damaged or dirty signs that negatively impact your image with visitors.

Regardless of sign quality, site signs usually are wasted money unless they are accompanied by appropriate landscaping. Whether your product is an entire community or a single home, expert landscaping is a key merchandising component integral to your image of high quality.

Landscaping Basics

Because of the permanent nature of most landscaping, its cost usually is included in the development budget rather than the marketing budget. Nevertheless, it is essential to product merchandising and should therefore be addressed in the marketing plan. The following guidelines are suggested for landscaping:

- Extend the property approach image as far as possible through landscaping to the community or lot boundary. Handsome landscaping proves more effective than signs in conveying an initial appealing image to prospects.
- Use mature plantings at the outset to convey an optimum image; young shrubs look sparse and cheap.
- Integrate walls, bulkheads, and other structural features, as well as water features (where feasible), with the overall landscaping plan.
- Carefully select plants to place below and beside signs that will not grow rapidly and reduce the sign's impact (an often neglected detail that mars many expensive entry presentations).
- Ensure that selected plantings will provide an optimum appearance during all seasons of the year.
- Incorporate seasonal flowers to create a fresh look and add occasional new eye appeal.
- Include the landscape architect early in the planning process to ensure optimum views from both inside and outside the model(s) and from the approach route.
- Include lighting to extend image presentation around the clock.

Amenities

Community amenities are an extension of landscaping that builders must carefully consider when they are developing or sharing in the development of a new community. Many questions arise when considering amenities: When should amenities be included? Which amenities are best for each situation? How much money should be allocated to amenities? Answers to these questions require careful analysis of consumer preferences and competitive offerings, and they have cost implications regarding product pricing.

The most common community amenities are pathways (including sidewalks), tennis courts, swimming pools, and clubhouses; others include playing fields, parks, play grounds, boating lakes, nature trails, exercise trails, golf courses, racquetball/squash courts, basketball courts, health clubs, and a host of special facilities normally designed to take advantage of distinctive site characteristics. A community amenity can be as small as a pathway with benches beside a pleasant stream or as major as a mountain with ski trails or a land preserve.

Natural Amenities

Natural amenities that are integral to a particular site (for example, a lake, stream, or mountain) add significant value and attractiveness to your site. Therefore, these amenities must be enhanced in some fashion to ensure that prospective purchasers fully appreciate them. Enhancement ideas include removing ground brush and low branches from a wooded area, adding a pathway or border landscaping to a lake or stream, or providing a seating area for a pleasant view.

Man-Made Amenities

Man-made amenities are generally optional cost-and-value additions that depend upon positioning for the targeted consumer rather than site enhancement. Effective merchandising presents any amenities included in an optimum fashion for appeal to the target consumers. Manmade amenities should be designed, developed, and located as part of the complete merchandising strategy because the number of purchasers who may be influenced to purchase a home because of these amenities will far exceed the number who will actually make regular use of them. For example buyers may visualize themselves swimming daily laps in the community pool but never dip their toes in the water after they move in. Therefore amenities must be designed for initial consumer appeal, developed at the outset as a showpiece, and located in a prominent position obvious to every site visitor— possibly even on the periphery property to attract passersby.

The promise of a community amenity on paper will not influence many prospects. If optimum positioning includes an amenity, it should be constructed first, making sure that it is distinctly attractive to the tastes of the primary target consumer group. Virtually every new home market in this country contains examples of communities that did not meet sales expectations because of deferred development of amenities. If they are shown on the plan, construct them at the outset of development.

Information Center

Whether it is called an information center, welcome center, visitor's center, model center, sales center, or sales office, its function is to provide an environment in which the builder's representatives (sales counselors) meet, inform, and sell prospective purchasers. Although sales center is the most common name for this facility, some have observed that information center sounds less intimidating to most prospects and therefore is a more comfortable space for them to enter.

By considering the critical elements—comfort, control, and closing (the Three Cs)—an information center can be tailored to each specific site and product, yet conform to recommended sales practices. The accompanying illustration (Figure 8.2) indicates the application of the Three Cs to a compact, highly successful information center accommodating one sales person (or two on weekends) in the double garage of a furnished model home. It incorporates the Three Cs of information center design with areas for closing and administrative functions separate from the display area.

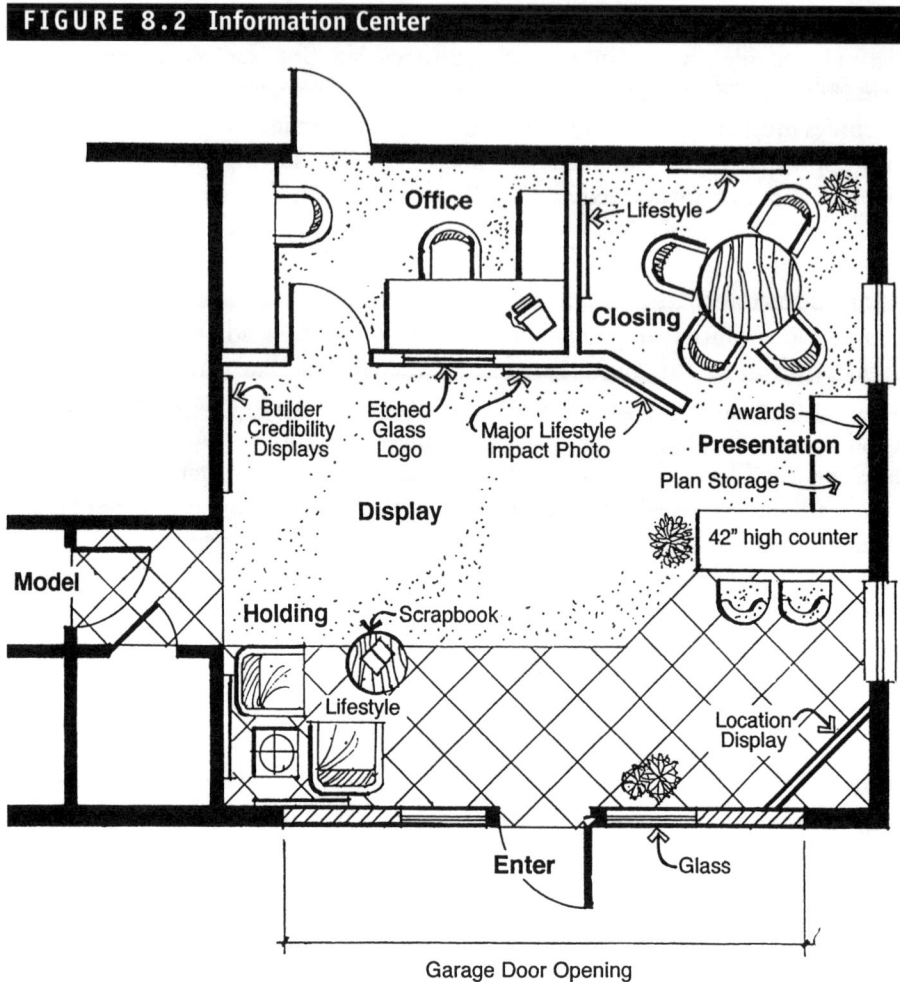

FIGURE 8.2 Information Center

Garage Door Opening

Comfort

Comfort is essential to successful information center design. Prospects must feel comfortable from the moment they drive onto the site. The merchandising steps at this stage include the items discussed in the following paragraphs:

Drive Entry and Parking. This building—clearly identified with a sign as the visitor's center or information center—should be visible from the nearest roadway and adjacent to an amenity whenever possible. It should convey no feeling of a trap. For example, fences around models to ensure visitors pass through the information center both before and after visiting the models are intimidating and uncomfortable for visitors. Builders in many markets continue the historical tradition of traps without visitor evaluation of the utility of this device. Individual builders who have omitted traps have achieved equal or higher success at lower cost. Parking should be arranged into separate sections (where feasible) for prospective customers and sales staff to ensure the maximum number of convenient parking spaces for visitors.

Walk, Entry, and Front Door. The front door should be clearly defined with an easy path to it. A glass front door allows visitors to see in and increases the light inside. Sliding doors are not as conducive to comfortable entry as a self-closing, hinged door. If the building must be raised substantially above existing grade, a series of decks is far preferable to a standard stairway. Of course, handicap access requires an optional ramp access for any stairway at a public entrance.

Display Area. In the display area, exhibits should present the lifestyle of the community through creative photography, renderings, and recreational symbols. Information graphics should include three sequential displays: a vicinity map for area orientation, a community plan for site orientation, and the developer and/or builder story. Additional displays often include the development team, key staff members, construction quality, special features, and floor plans and elevations are often included. But the authors believe that floor plans and elevations are best examined with a sales counselor seated at a table where a dialogue can be initiated toward purchase commitments. Do not display sufficient detailed information for a consumer to reach a negative decision, instead motivate visitors to ask a sales counselor for information.

The exhibits should be enticing enough to occupy prospects for a few minutes when a sales counselor is not immediately available.

Traditionally builders have displayed plans and elevations of new home offerings in visitor information centers. Some builders use the available display space for this purpose to the exclusion of lifestyle photographs and other information graphics. Builders using displays predominantly of house plans assumed that consumers examined these plans to compare competitive offerings. But increasing numbers of builders have realized that most consumers rely upon three-dimensional model homes for comparison rather than floor plans, which few of them can really understand. Furthermore, consumers tend to be more interested in neighborhood and community attributes prior to home selection. Therefore, in future years you can expect to see a decreasing emphasis on floor plan displays as increasing numbers of builders focus on creating selling environments with emotional appeal for visitors, including the use of computer virtual reality addressed later in this chapter.

The credibility of the developer and/or builder is essential information for prospective purchasers. Chapter 5 presents a builder credibility statement for a Pennsylvania developer-builder.

Control

Control is the second C of information center design. In order to achieve both control and comfort, you need to avoid intimidating physical visitor traps, and you should screen any semblance of an office environment from the display area, preferably keep the office in a separate room or work area.

Work Stations. Sales counselors' work areas should allow unobtrusive monitoring of visitor activity while hiding paperwork. You also need to provide separate closing or discussion areas. The separate administration work area requires good lighting and individual privacy areas, plus ample storage for sales counselors (no prospect visitors). The consumer discussion area is described below as the closing room.

Exhibits. The sales person should be able to focus the visitor's attention on one exhibit at a time—with no distractions. The exit from the exhibits should be toward views of amenities or models.

Literature. At the end of the tour the counselors should offer floor plans, lifestyle brochures, and related printed material (such as lists of municipal amenities, schools, recreation facilities, shopping , and the like). A literature storage area should be conveniently accessible to the sales person near the exit from the exhibits. Sales brochures should not be left on display for anyone to take; they should be treated as valued information for personal presentation.

View Area and Exit to Models. The view area is a designated location for discussion of the development within view of amenities. The primary goal is to get the visitor into the model homes; therefore, this area should not be designed for comfortable sitting. The exit to the models should be through another self-closing glass door (not a sliding door) onto a small deck or patio—a brief holding area—where feasible. Steps and walkways to models should be wide enough for three adults to walk side-by-side. The appearance of your models is discussed in the next section of this chapter.

Return from the Models. The exit to the models also functions as an impressive entrance when visitors return from the models. Exhibits now should be more meaningful to the prospect. If the sales person believes that it is time to get down to business, he or she should lead the visitor(s) to the closing room. Otherwise a few additional moments in the viewing area will set up the programmed exit routine, including distribution of literature.

Closing

Closing is the most important of the Three Cs. Once a sales counselor initiates a closing, it should not be interrupted. The information center must incorporate the following features to support the closing process.

Route to Closing Room. This route should be quick and direct to avoid any sense of being trapped.

Closing Room. This room is becoming increasingly used for discussions of consumer needs prior to the tour, therefore it is also called a discussion room in addition to a closing room. It should provide plenty of natural light, as well as views of landscape features or amenities. However, the windows should not provide views of potential distractions. The room or rooms should accommodate a round table 42 inches in diameter and four comfortable chairs (provide activities for children outside the closing room.) Additional lifestyle photos may be on display here. The closing room should be in full view of the view area, but acoustically private. (The doors should close.)

Increasingly, sales counselors are using personal computers in the selling process, both for financing details and for product display such as virtual reality tours described below. To accommodate a computer in closing or discussion rooms, the round table is being replaced with keyhole shaped tables that offer the comfort of a round table and include a location for the computer. Figure 8.3 illustrates an information center equipped with such tables.

Virtual Reality

During the past decade several firms developed computer simulations of model homes to support the selling process. The traditional reliance upon floor plans and written descriptions of options has always proven inferior to presenting fully merchandised model homes. Now, with the advent of three-dimensional computer simulations, commonly termed virtual reality, builders can present a variety of models plus options for each model in a full-color computer format.

According to Steve G. Ormonde, president of Ormonde Presentations of California and Florida, "a builder can have blueprints converted into high-quality, photo-realistic virtual model homes at a fraction of the cost of building and merchandising full-scale model homes. In addition, virtual models can demonstrate just about every combination of options and upgrades, which is impossible with their physical counterparts." Ormonde says that virtual reality generates increased profits and leads to more satisfied homeowners. The prospective purchaser thus

FIGURE 8.3 Information Center: Use of Keyhole-Shape Tables

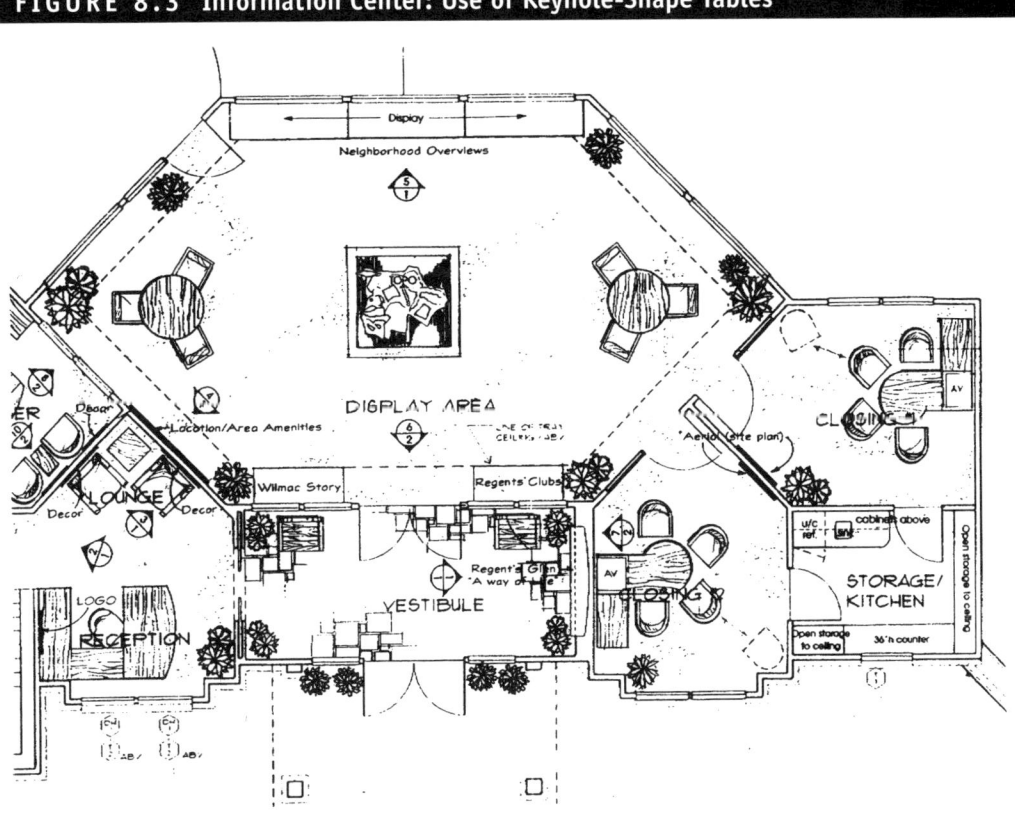

Courtesy of Gart Urban Associates, Miami, Florida.

can visualize every aspect of the new home prior to construction. Figure 8.4 illustrates a virtual reality computer simulation of a furnished model home from Ormonde Presentations.

Selection Room

The model center also requires a selection center in a separate location from the visitor information center. (Sometimes it is off-site in a central location for multisite builders.)

Model Merchandising

The purpose of model merchandising is to present your homes to visitors in the most appealing manner. A model home should enable prospective purchasers to—

- see, touch, and smell the features
- learn how those features will become benefits to buyers when they purchase
- visualize how their happiness will be increased by living in the home

Exterior Merchandising

Whereas many professionals specialize in model interiors, the exterior customarily is defined by the architect, residential designer, or builder. The exterior is a key

FIGURE 8.4 Virtual Reality Computer Simulation of Model Home

merchandising component for an early impression on the visiting consumer, and you should provide as much attention to it, particularly the front elevation, as to the model interior.

Model exterior materials and colors should complement other components of the site elements and the marketing theme. Chapter 7 provides advice on colors is provided—a vital element of your overall presentation. Mature-growth landscaping further supports a strong initial impression.

The orientation of the model is an equally vital element of your overall presentation. Its relationship to afternoon sun in different seasons can ensure strong color enhancement, or alternatively emphasize negative window and patio exposure. Of perhaps greatest importance is ensuring that your model's front elevation is the initial image for the visitor. Model lot orientations that provide a rear or side view from the approach road will negate all your attention to the front facade.

Interior Merchandising

Model merchandising enhances the appearance of a home to elicit a positive emotional response from prospective purchasers. It supports the oral sales presentation through sensory communication of comfort and style and thereby induces perceived value beyond that possible with an empty house. Effective interior merchandising has nothing to do with selling furniture, drapery, carpeting, or accessories. The underlying objective of interior merchandising is to create the illusion of living in this home. It emphasizes the positive features of the home while downplaying negative ones. Successful merchandisers carefully select furnishings, coverings, and accessories compatible with the tastes and financial resources of target consumers. Furnishings beyond the budgets of prospective purchasers will spoil the illusion just as cheap furnishings will turn off affluent prospects. Thus, you must provide your merchandiser with a concise description of the target consumer for each model home.

According to Patti Guthrie of Marc-Michaels Interior Design in Winter Park, Florida: "A good merchandiser creates the urgency to move. Most buyers don't have to move right now. It is our job to create that urgency by showing prospects furnishings they can envision owning in future." Guthrie also points out that most new home prospects visit 10 communities with two or three models each. "Your model home must have high impact upon entry and memory points throughout to be remembered."

A high proportion of any builder's prospects visit models as their initial introduction to the builder and his or her product offerings, therefore the model interior is the critical product display. It is an investment in revenue generation.

Merchandising Alternatives. Alternatives vary from the age-old option of doing nothing (on the grounds that purchasers will be suspect of the proportion of house cost spent on marketing) to elaborate model interiors costing up to 2 or 3 percent of development sales revenues. The industry standard is 25 to 30 percent of the home's selling price. As in most marketing components, economies of scale clearly allow large-volume builders to present merchandised models at a lower percentage of revenues than small-volume builders can manage. However, if your competition is well merchandised, you may need to increase the budget allocation for merchandising accordingly.

Three Options. Other than simply cleaning up a speculative house and offering it for inspection, builders have three options:

- full furnishings by a professional model merchandiser (no novices or furniture store displays, that can cause critical color and space errors that negatively impact your visitors)
- selective vignette merchandising, which highlights furnishings, window treatments, accessories (or variations of the enhancements that usually depend on the home buyer's budget)
- interior wall décor complemented with potted plants

If budget limitations prohibit a fully furnished interior, eliminate the furnishings and concentrate on floor and wall coverings coupled with professional color coordination and selective accessories—a "shell" model. Selective displays of furnishings in key rooms or master bedrooms often enhance this approach. Prospects are invited to imagine how they would furnish remaining spaces.

Of course, these alternatives are in descending order of cost and consumer impact. Patti Guthrie also suggests the option of a beautifully framed floor plan and/or color rendering of a key room prepared by a professional merchandiser. This enables your buyer to see how their furnishings will actually work in the space.

In general, more expensive products and products targeted to more mature and sophisticated consumers require higher allocations for merchandising than lower price products designed for first-time purchasers or first move-up purchasers. On the other hand, more sophisticated purchasers may better visualize the appearance of alternative floor plans from a single model, whereas less experienced consumers may need to see and touch a nearly exact replica of the home they intend to purchase (requiring models of additional available dwelling plans).

Some builders prefer to include signs in models explaining which items are options, decorator items, and part of the base price. However, such signs conflict with the ambiance created by the professional merchandiser. The merchandiser produces an interior to enhance the dwelling design and stimulate the emotions of the visitor. Explanatory signs (including business cards and other designer promotions) detract from this environment and create a retail store impression. You can give your sales counselors the responsibility of explaining interior features and benefits rather than overconcern yourself with explanations for unescorted traffic.

New homes will not sell themselves and visual signs or audio aids, either wall speakers or personal cassettes, will not replace human contact. Model merchandising supports the personal selling process. It is not in lieu of this process.

Re-Accessorize. For models that are beginning to appear worn, or for a shift in the consumer market, you can achieve a fresh look by having your merchandiser re-accessorize them. Purchasing new accessories is relatively economical, yet they can produce a dramatic change in the model interior.

Find the Right Merchandiser

Finding the merchandiser for a particular market and budget is another step in your seemingly never-ending search for talent. The merchandiser chosen should boast substantial training and experience in model interior merchandising, particularly in the housing type and price range you are offering. (Preferably the merchandiser should be a member of the American Society of Interior Designers.) The merchandiser should be a proven detail person. You should check the merchandisers sample models for the small details, such as accessorized closet and cabinet installations. Communications and interpersonal chemistry are also important factors—the builder should look for the type of person he or she can interact with and who exhibits flexibility in finding alternative solutions. As with other team members, confirm references for a potential merchandiser. Most past clients should be willing to hire that merchandiser again.

You should retain the merchandiser as part of the design team for input to home design prior to finalizing floor plans. No matter when you hire one you should request proposals from one or more merchandisers (but not more than three) and make certain that each receives identical market research information and house plans.

Evaluate Merchandising

Evaluation is essential to selecting and getting the best work from a merchandiser. Each professional merchandiser will present different creative solutions for a given opportunity. Creativity cannot be evaluated by mathematical criteria or objective checklists. Although you will want to know the criteria that indicate successful model merchandisers. For example, a successful merchandiser ensures that window treatments cover no more than 15 percent of the window surface to ensure space-enhancing natural light. Success is judged on emotional appeal generated in target consumers—the achievement of style and attitude that sets a model apart from competition and leaves visitors with a memorable experience.

The principles described in the following paragraphs should guide a successful relationship with any merchandiser.

Define the Target Group. The merchandiser should first insist upon a target consumer definition and then design an interior expressly for that group. In the case of more than one target group and only one model, the merchandiser and builder (and other appropriate team members) should decide on the best target group for merchandising. The merchandiser can appeal to secondary target groups with a color scheme and theme that appeals to most people.

Consistency. Consistency is vital throughout the marketing program and must be pursued diligently in merchandising. Consumers who respond to an advertisement with a colonial American theme should not arrive to find a model interior in art deco style. The information center color scheme should not clash with colors in the model interior. As noted above, the merchandiser should coordinate the interior colors and finishes with the exterior and landscaping materials.

Selling Homes. You should adhere to the basic principles of merchandising to be sure that the primary objective remains selling homes, not furniture or appliances. The interior decor must complement home spaces, benefits, and features. Colors, fabrics, and furniture should reinforce strengths and minimize shortcomings. Natural light and exterior vistas should shine through windows, with no signs or messages detracting from the emotional image being created. A sample model interior appears in Figure 8.4.

Budget. Establishing—and adhering to—a budget is the mark of a professional. Any deviation without prior agreement is unprofessional.

Electronic Merchandising

The increasing use of virtual reality presentations of model homes raises the issue of decisions on electronically merchandised interiors. Virtual reality suppliers should retain an experienced model home merchandiser on staff to translate consumer characteristics and preferences into interior decor. Alternatively, you may need to retain a model merchandiser to consult with the virtual reality supplier to ensure competent selection of interiors. In either event, the virtual reality tour should meet the criteria of this chapter and in particular the principle of model merchandising that supports the personal selling process.

Conclusion

To produce winning results, establish initial rapport between you, the builder, and the merchandiser and couple expressions of confidence with objective critiques throughout the design process. Professional merchandisers know that their success is inextricably interwoven with their builder-client's success, and they will perform accordingly to achieve the common goal of increasing sales through cost-effective marketing.

III

MONITOR

Monitor means to learn from experience through collecting and analyzing of consumer response. Marketing communications are continuing experiments that you can evaluate by tracking the numbers of persons responding and the specific opinions of respondents about the marketing communications.

Evaluate Marketing Performance

Marketing activities generate new consumers who initiate the selling process with established opinions about the builder and builder's new homes based marketing communications. The number of consumers generated can indicate marketing cost-effectiveness and the consumers' opinions provide a performance measure for marketing activities and expenditures.

This final chapter describes essential marketing evaluation information in terms of collection and use. This evaluation information comes from your consumers, first from short questionnaires answered by inquiring consumers and second from more detailed questionnaires and focus groups involving purchasers. It also can come from purchasers of your competitor's homes. Efficiently summarizing and analyzing this information on a regular basis provides objective guidelines for improving your marketing program.

Value of Numbers

Builders commonly use visitor registration cards or marketing questionnaires, particularly those builders operating information centers and/or model homes. This practice has been gaining acceptance over many decades as builders increasingly recognized the need for more information about their consumers to use in individual follow-up communications, as well as to guide future marketing decisions. The follow-up selling process is essential to sales success, but this book focuses on information on marketing new homes.

Processing consumer information used to be a lengthy and monotonous task, but the advent of personal computers has reduced information summarization to a simple input operation. Several companies now produce specialized software for processing this information concurrently with prospect tracking and follow-up communications. It also makes mortgage loan calculations and explores financing options. According to Pat Brennan, president of Tampa-based Maxim Data, "more medium-sized and even small-volume builders are using automated sales support systems." He expects this trend to continue as personal computers become an accepted support mechanism for salespersons as well as administrative staff.

Site visitors and even telephone contacts will answer questions on current location (origin), age, marital status, household size, current tenure, household income, purchase reason, time looking, and source of awareness of your development. They can indicate preferences for dwelling type, price, bedrooms, and size. In addition to providing valuable follow-up information for your sales counselors, summarizing this data from many consumers provides profile information for designing and modifying marketing programs.

For example, the three graphs of information on site visitors in Figure 9.1 show substantial shifts in consumer age, income, and desired price range from 1996 to 1998 in response to advertising for new higher price products. Had these shifts to consumers looking for higher-priced housing not occurred, modifications to advertising would be appropriate to stimulate visits from consumers interested in such housing.

Of perhaps greater importance is comparing profile data on visitors with comparable profile data on actual purchasers. As illustrated in Figure 9.2, one-fourth of purchasers in the sample development were assisted by a real estate agent whereas only half that ratio of visitors reported assistance from a real estate agent. In this case, the builder should shift greater marketing attention to activities to increase real estate agent awareness of the development and to reinforce the actual behavior characteristics of the purchasers.

Figure 9.3 illustrates a sample analysis of marketing cost-effectiveness for a specific development. The builder's staff recorded all consumer inquiries according to the source of awareness indicated by that consumer. The staff also recorded costs of marketing communications for the same sources. Cost per inquiry is thus calculated as a measure of cost-effectiveness of specific communications media. Of course, some expenditures may not generate inquiries in the same month, and therefore the cumulative quarterly and annual calculations would prove more relevant.

Many consumers appear to remember advertising better than publicity articles so expenditures on public relations may not be rewarded with as many responses as other media, even though in-depth interviews with consumers often reveal publicity articles as stronger motivators than advertisements. Regardless of the interpretation you apply to these numbers, you must collect the numbers and summarize them as a basis for performance evaluation.

Rigorous and regular attention to these answers to key questions will provide valuable insights to marketing expenditures. Modifications may produce higher cost-effectiveness as marketing expenditures generate more qualified consumers.

FIGURE 9.1 Site Visitor Survey

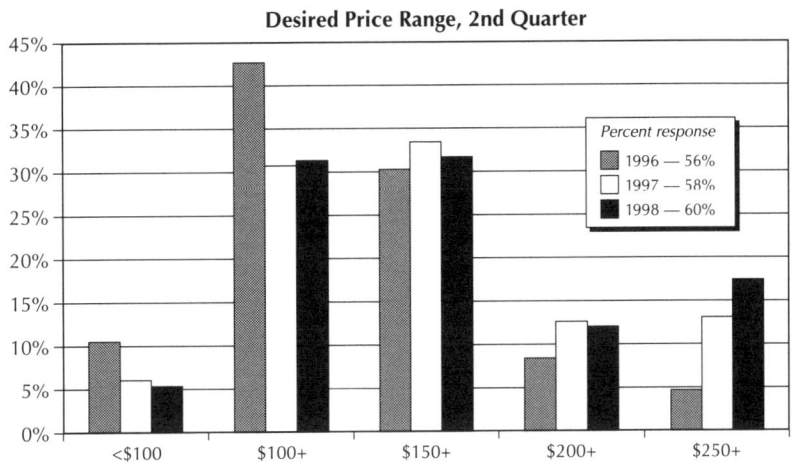

Desired Price Range, 2nd Quarter

Percent response
1996 — 56%
1997 — 58%
1998 — 60%

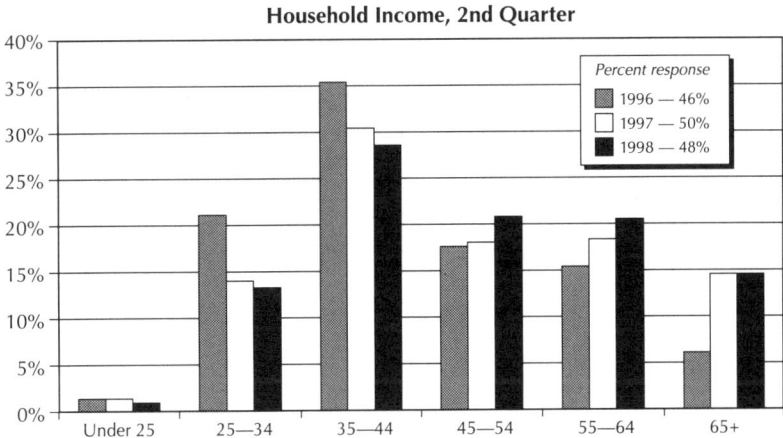

Household Income, 2nd Quarter

Percent response
1996 — 46%
1997 — 50%
1998 — 48%

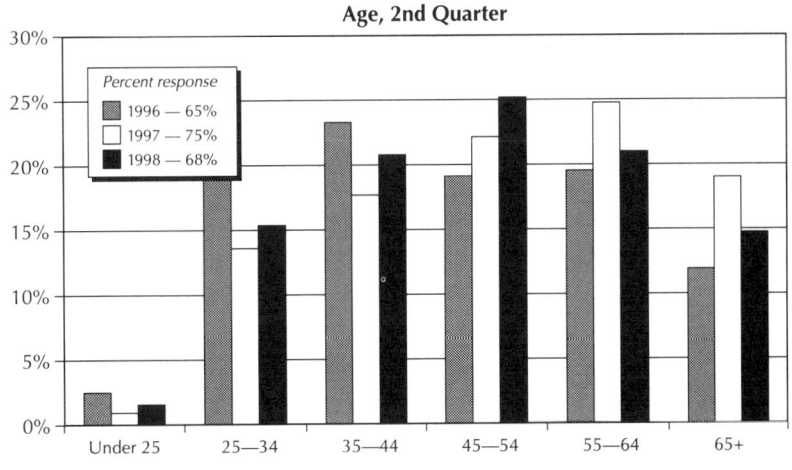

Age, 2nd Quarter

Percent response
1996 — 65%
1997 — 75%
1998 — 68%

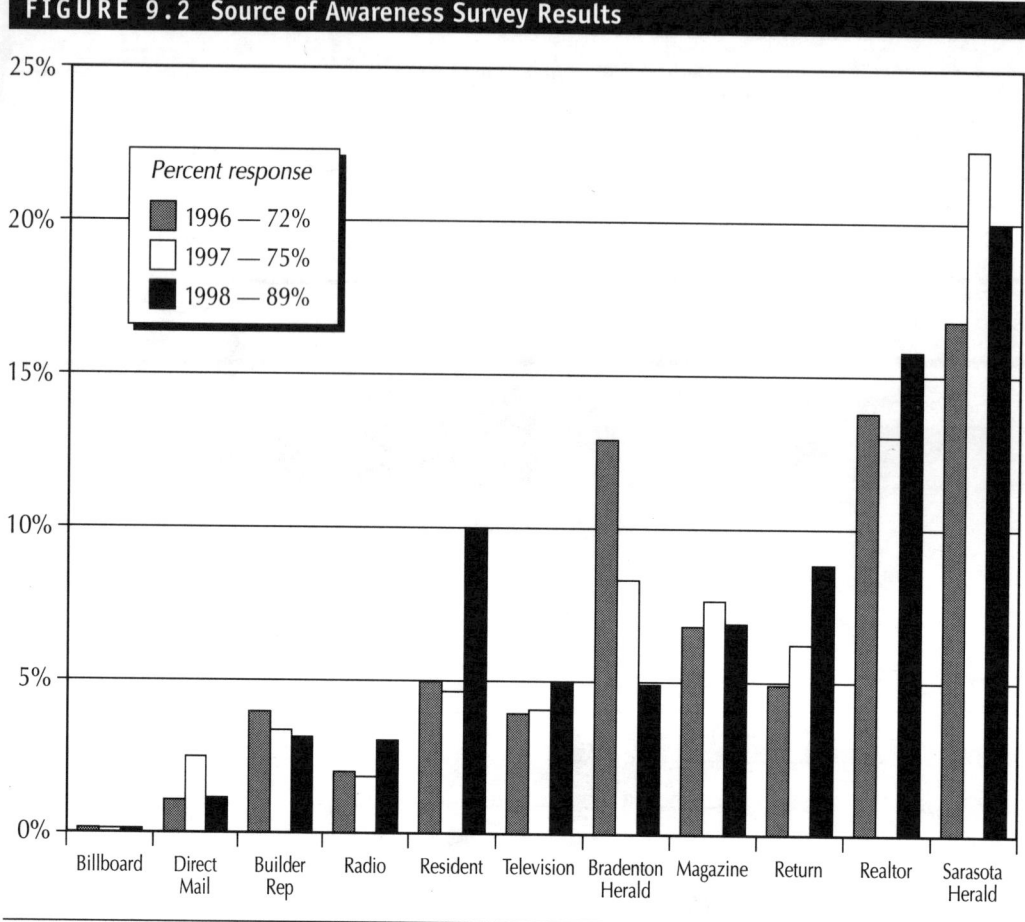

FIGURE 9.2 Source of Awareness Survey Results

Successful builders review this summary information at least quarterly, and some do it on a monthly basis.

Value of Consumer Opinions

Consumers (possible purchasers) are the best source of information about housing preferences; levels of satisfaction with your homes; preferred product benefits, features, and designs; marketing and sales effectiveness; and product presentation. Although many builders take pride in their remarkable intuition about consumer needs and preferences, most require structured advice from consumers. By discovering the needs, wants, and desires of new home consumers, builders can respond with plans and features designed accordingly. Better-targeted products coupled with accurate marketing communications will generate greater profits. Figure 9.4 presents an example of a visitor information card.

Although everyone has opinions, and most people are willing to share their opinions, only opinions from selected groups of consumers are useful to builders: (a) prospective new home purchasers actively shopping for a new home in the

FIGURE 9.3 Sample Marketing Cost-Effectiveness					
	For the Month			**Year to Date**		
	Inquiries	**Cost**	**Cost/Inquiry**	**Inquirys**	**Cost**	**Cost/Inquiry**
Newspapers	42	$13,410	$319.29	388	$72,372	$186.53
Magazines	0	0	0	0	0	NA
Radio/TV	3	0	0	3	991	330.33
Outdoor signs	102	5,290	51.86	603	33,527	55.60
Direct mail	0	0	NA	0	0	NA
Support ads (e.g. Resort)	0	0	NA	0	0	NA
Public relations	0	1,346	NA	1	6,579	6,579.00
Promotions	0	0	NA	0	0	NA
Referrals	14	0	0.00	129	0	0.00
Agent	35	0	0.00	204	0	0.00
Self-prospecting	0	0	NA	9	0	0.00
Resort guest	0	0	NA	0	0	NA
Other advertising costs						
Ad agency fees	0	3,675	NA	0	22,125	NA
General advertising	0	2,305	NA	0	10,517	NA
Ad production	0	275	NA	0	11,817	NA
	196	$23,301	$134.19	$1,337	$157,928	$118.12
Other marketing costs						
Product merchandising	0	1,082	NA	0	23,255	NA
Market control	0	2,500	NA	0	15,000	NA
Marketing Total	**196**	**$29,883**	**$152.46**	**1,337**	**$196,183**	**$146.73**

target price range, (b) purchasers of your new homes, and (c) purchasers of competitors' new homes.

Prospective New Home Purchasers

The most accessible prospective new home purchasers are visitors to your information center. The visitor information card in Figure 9.4 is the normal means of gaining information from these visitors. Most builders present this card to new visitors as the price of admission—"Please fill out this registration card before I introduce a sales counselor to you." You can obtain much more accurate information by having the sales counselor write down, or type in, the information as a part of the introductory discussion during the selling process—a technique rejected by some salespeople as unnecessary work, when in fact it can be a successful relationship-building activity in a comfortable sitting position rather than the normal standing introduction. Experienced sales counselors for retirement communities are accustomed to this method of initiating the selling process with persons who often are physically uncomfortable standing up.

You can supplement information on the visitor card with exit surveys administered by an independent surveyor as visitors leave the information center at the end of the selling process. These surveys usually are limited to six or eight questions on

FIGURE 9.4 Visitor Information Card

Lakewood Ranch
The Nature Of Florida Living.

Visitor Survey

Name _____ Date _____

Mailing Address_____ City _____

State _____ Zip _____ Occupation _____

Home Phone (_____)_____ Other Phone (_____)_____

Comments _____
_____
_____
_____
_____

(Continued on other side)

Marital Status
___Married ___Divorced ___Single ___Widowed

Family Size
_1 _2 _3 _4 _5 or more

Family Income
_ $20-40,000 ___ $70-100,000 ___Over $200,000
_ $40-55,000 ___ $100-150,000
_ $55-70,000 ___ $150-200,000

Current Residence
___Own ___Rent Monthly payment or rent $_____

Desired Occupancy In
_ 0-6 Months _ 6-9 Months _ 3-6 Months _ Over 9 Months

Type of Property Desired
_ Single-story detached _Two-story detached
_ Townhouse _Custom Home
Condominium

Desired Number of Bedrooms
_ 2 or less _ 3 _ 4 _ 5 or more

Square Footage Desired
Under 1,300 sq. ft. 1,600-2,000 sq. ft. Over 2,500 sq. ft
1,301-1,600 sq. ft 2,001-2,500 sq. ft.
Price Range Desired
___Under $100,000 ___$150,001-200,000
___$100,001-001-150,000 ___$200,001-250250,000
___Over 250,000

Do you need to sell before purchasing? Yes___ No___
What prompted your visit?
_____

Reason For Buying
_Relocating   _Retiring   _Investment
_Smaller Home   _Bigger Home   _Location
_Other _____
Which item or items brought Lakewood Ranch to
your attention:
_ Radio: _____   _ Realtor _____
_ TV: _____   _ Sarasota Herald
_ Direct mail   _ Bradenton Herald
_ Drive By   _ Magazine:_____
_ Return visit   _ Other:_____
_ Builder Reputation _____

---

a single page with the answers recorded by the person asking the questions. They are particularly useful in evaluating the selling process while the experience is still fresh. Figure 1.12 presents an example of a new home visitor exit survey.

The visitor follow-up survey is another useful supplement to visitor cards. You mail a questionnaire of up to two pages in length and no more than 20 questions with an incentive for responding. Alternatively you can conduct this survey by telephone with a higher response rate. These follow-up surveys have lower response rates than person-to-person exit surveys, but more information can be collected from each survey questionnaire. Follow-up surveys also can evaluate the selling process. In addition, they serve as a continuation of the selling process by keeping the consumer aware of your community in anticipation of a second visit. Survey design is described below.

Although the information collected by these surveys of prospective purchasers contains qualitative answers, they are answers that often can be structured into a set of opinions for subsequent numeric summary. In short, you even can analyze qualitative opinions to guide management decisions on future marketing.

Your New Home Owners

As with the visitor research described above, you can solicit cost-effectiveness information from your new homeowners. In addition to providing reliable information, your owners will be more likely to refer other prospects to you if you take a genuine interest in their opinions.

Owners of your new homes have a stronger interest in providing information to you than consumers who have not purchased a home from you. They are more likely to respond to requests for opinions. Of course, they may want to express negative concerns that require attention to support purchaser satisfaction. But they also will reveal the positive reasons that motivated their purchases.

Surveys of new home purchasers can be conducted in person, by telephone, or by mail. Mail is the most economical, but it does not generate as high a response rate as personal or telephone interviews. You should phrase the questions so they provide you insights into the following:

- housing needs
- levels of satisfaction
- product features and designs
- marketing effectiveness
- sales presentation performance

Their opinions are particularly valuable within 30 to 45 days after they purchase a home. A second follow-up survey conducted about a year after purchase provides a useful comparison with the initial follow-up survey, particularly if the second questionnaire emanates from an independent source, such as a market research company. Thus, the new owner follow-up survey has dual purposes: It informs the new resident that you are vitally interested in purchaser satisfaction as well as opinions, and it collects facts and opinions for management's information and use.

The second survey has the primary purpose of collecting independent opinions from the residents without bias from those who might like to communicate directly with the builder about complaints or other issues.

Survey Design. Professionals should design both of these surveys in accordance with the particular needs and circumstances of each builder. However, a builder can normally use the initial design several years of questioning. Figure 1.13 presents a successful homeowner survey.

Surveying Procedures. Once questionnaires have been designed for both the 30- to 45-day new owner follow-up survey and the 1-year survey, you should distribute the surveys and analyze them as follows:

- Establish a tickler file by week or month that extends over a 2-year period. At closing, insert into this file the two survey packages for each new owner. Each package should contain a survey questionnaire and cover letter from you or your market research firm (if applicable), plus a stamped return envelope addressed to either you or the market research firm (1-year survey).
- Make a clerical person on your staff responsible for mailing the envelopes from the tickler file each week or month throughout the year.
- Collect and submit responses from the 30- to 45-day survey in bulk to the market research organization semi-annually or annually (annually for builders with 50 or fewer sales) or maintain an internal tabulation and analysis with spreadsheet software on your computer. Similarly collect, tabulate, and analyze responses from the 1-year survey annually.
- Computer tabulation and analysis of completed questionnaires normally requires a month. Therefore you should schedule the analysis prior to completion of your annual marketing plan and budget—for example, questionnaire tabulation and analysis in November for marketing plan and budget preparation in December of each year.

If you complete the analysis of both surveys simultaneously, you can compare responses on similar types of questions. In addition, both types of information provide valuable input to the annual marketing plan and budget process.

Your Competitor's Purchasers

Prospects who may have visited your model homes, but purchased a competitor's product, may provide even more valuable information for you than your own purchasers. Many people tend to support their own decisions, and therefore your purchasers may not be completely objective in their responses to you. But people who investigated your offerings and then purchased elsewhere are a valuable resource for criticism about your products and marketing.

You can identify your competitor's purchasers by address listings and survey them in person, by telephone, or by mail using questions virtually identical to those posed to your new homeowners. By keeping the questions similar in the two types of surveys, you can readily compare answers.

Focus Groups

Using focus groups to provide consumer input for planning, design, and marketing decisions is becoming widespread in the homebuilding industry. The purpose of such groups is to elicit opinions on one or more topics through a structured discussion among targeted consumers. Although you may want a professional discussion leader, many builders gather groups of their homeowners together informally to focus on current issues requiring policy decisions. They gain new insights from the people who are experiencing the livability of their new homes.

Real estate agents also can be focus group participants to provide helpful critiques of new home offerings. In addition, builders frequently ask their own sales staff to interact with real estate agents in such focus groups and also to participate in separate focus groups. Sharing videotapes of consumer focus groups with your sales staff can stimulate their ideas as well as keep them informed about consumer concerns and preferences.

The design and implementation of focus groups is described in Chapter 1 along with other market research techniques.

Marketing Management Reports

Many builders do not have the time or inclination to examine the detailed information on performance evaluations. They require staff or consultant reports that summarize marketing performance indicators from efficient computer programs and receive brief evaluations on a regular basis. The frequency of such reports varies with the perceived needs of each home builder—weekly, monthly, quarterly—but the marketing manager must be prepared for information requests on short notice at any time.

In addition to sales activity reports, home builders require four types of marketing performance reports: visitor response, cost-effectiveness, owner surveys, and competition.

Visitor Response

Visitor response reports summarize the number of visitors per reporting period and their characteristics as described in Figures 9.1 and 9.2. These reports require a brief interpretation of the visitor data with particular emphasis on changes since the previous report. If such changes are consistent with planned product and marketing shifts, you can claim success. If not, you may need to make additional modifications.

Cost-Effectiveness

The annual marketing plan includes specific or implied costs for attracting each visitor. Thus, the cost of marketing to attract consumers divided by the number of visitors during a specified time period provides a cost figure to compare with planning objectives and measure cost-effectiveness.

Some builders attempt to include only "qualified" visitors in evaluating the effectiveness of marketing to attract consumers. However, this refinement relies upon the ability of sales persons to qualify visitors through questions, and this ability varies widely among sales persons and among markets. Furthermore, sales persons who are judged on how well they convert qualified visitors have a natural incentive to limit the reported numbers of such visitors, and thereby cause a possible superficial reduction of marketing cost-effectiveness. With the possible exception of initial grand opening events that attract curiosity seekers, many builders find that a consistent count of all visitors works better as a measure of marketing cost-effectiveness.

Owner Surveys

These reports to management are similar to the above-mentioned reports in that they summarize the answers to survey questions, compare them to prior trends, interpret the results, and use them to guide possible modification of product designs and marketing. The frequency of these reports depends upon the scale of each builder's operation. If you build 20 homes annually, an owner survey report once per year should be sufficient. But, if you are building 200 homes per year, you need quarterly reports to keep current on changing needs and marketing concerns.

Competition

Regularly monitoring the operations of competitive builders also provides essential comparative performance information. Some builders plot the locations of competitors on a wall map and examine their product design, prices, value ratios, features, monthly sales, and marketing actions in comparison with their own operations. They would include in their performance information on their competitors subjective performance criteria such as quality of the competitor's sales staff and the local consumers' perception of the value of the dwelling area and features.

Builder Management

Managing a building company involves coordinating marketing, sales, and other activities through periodic planning and budgeting. Regular sales performance and marketing reports assist this process. This supplementary information is essential to decision-making about planning and budgeting.

Regardless of how many people are involved in the generation of this information (although in a small organization, it might involve only two or three people with overlapping responsibilities), they need to make management decisions on strategic planning for future activities efficiently and confidently.

Make Marketing Happen

Many builders spend a great deal of their time on unexpected issues requiring immediate attention and therefore have limited time to implement the marketing procedures described in this book. This last section presents a rapid action method of implementing a sound marketing system in a 1-day exercise.

You can apply this 1-day marketing audit to a building operation of any scale to analyze shortcomings and plan improvements. To conduct this audit you need to complete each of the steps listed in Figure 9.5.

FIGURE 9.5 *One-Day Marketing Audit*

- Reserve at least a full day to conduct a thorough examination of marketing activities.

- Organize the diagnostic review using the three phases and nine components of the new homes marketing system described in the Introduction to this book.

- For each component, assemble all relevant information available. For example, collect samples of all advertising over the past 2 years, as well as expenditures for that advertising, any plans or proposals for additional advertising, and reports of results of that advertising in terms of inquiries generated and sales achieved.

- Critically examine activities conducted within each component of the system and compare them to the prescriptive guidelines provided in this book. Note successes and shortcomings.

- Document one or more concise, recommended actions for improving each component.

- Examine each recommendation in terms of the need for professional marketing expertise. Can you implement a recommendation inhouse or does it require an external specialist?

- Examine each recommendation with respect to urgency and assign a priority of 1, 2, 3, 4 or A, B, C, D.

- In consultation with senior staff and appropriate consultants, reexamine priorities to provide a realistic balance in each category and to serve as a basis for an action program.

- Establish a preliminary action program to achieve each of the recommendations in order of priority over a reasonable time period of weeks, months, or even years.

- Solicit proposals from selected external specialists for those recommendations which you have indicated require such assistance.

- Reschedule your action program for improving marketing and sales according to achievable cost and time guidelines.

- Begin implementing those recommendations assigned urgent priority status.

- Regularly monitor progress in implementing the action program.

- Finally, make marketing happen.

Selected
Bibliography

Alreck, Pamela L., and Robert B. Settle. *The Survey Research Handbook: Guidelines and Strategies for Conducting a Survey.* 2nd ed. Chicago: Irwin Professional Publishing, 1995.

Ambry, Margaret. *The Almanac of Consumer Markets: A Demographic Guide to Finding Today's Complex and Hard-to-Reach Customers.* Ithaca, N.Y.: American Demographics Press, 1990.

"Ask Consumers First: Focus Groups, Proxy Opinion Surveys Make Research Easier, More Affordable." *Southeast Homebuilder and Remodeler* (December 1992): 14–15.

Bade, Nicholas E. *Marketing Without Money: 175 Free, Cheap and Offbeat Ways for Small Business to Increase Sales!* Willoughby, Ohio: Halle House Publishing, 1993.

Barabba, Vincent P., and Gerald Zaltmann. *Hearing the Voice of the Market: Competitive Advantage Through Creative Use of Market Information.* Cambridge, Mass.: Harvard Business School Press, 1991.

"Blocking and Tackling: Essential Fundamentals to Success." *Monthly Marketing Ideas* (March/April, 1994): 2–3.

Crispell, Diane, ed. *The Insider's Guide to Demographic Know-How: How to Find, Analyze, and Use Information About Your Customers.* 3rd ed. Ithaca, N. Y.: American Demographics Press, 1993.

Elkman, Richard L. *Building Better Ads: New Home Advertising That Works.* 4th ed.: Washington, D.C.: Home Builder Press, 1996.

Goodman, Raymond J. Jr., and Douglas Smith. *Retirement Facilities: Planning Design, and Marketing.* New York: Watson-Gupthill Publications, 1992.

Hebert, John A., and William R. Smolkin. *Building for the Market.* Washington, D.C.: National Association of Home Builders, 1993.

How to Build Your Image with Community Involvement. Washington, D.C.: National Association of Home Builders, 1995.

Hughes, James W., and George Sternlieb. *The Dynamics of America's Housing.* Brunswick, NJ: Center For Urban Policy Research, 1987.

Koelsch, Frank. *The Informedia Revolution: How It Is Changing Our World and Your Life.* Toronto: McGraw-Hill Ryerson, 1995.

Lessinger, Jack. *Penturbia: Where Real Estate Will Boom After the Crash of Suburbia.* Seattle: SocioEconomics, Inc. 1990.

Levinson, Jay Conrad. *Guerrilla Marketing: Secrets for Making Big Profits from Your Small Business.* Boston: Houghton Mifflin, 1993.

Linneman, Robert, and John L. Stanton. *Making Niche Marketing Work: How to Grow Bigger* by Acting Smaller. New York: McGraw-Hill, 1991.

Longino, Charles F. Jr. *Retirement Migration In America.* Houston: Vacation Publications, 1995.

McLean, Mary L., and Kenneth P. Voyteck. *Understandng Your Economy: Using Analysis to Guide Local Strategic Planning.* Chicago: Planners Press, 1992.

Mitchell, Jan. *Sales and Marketing Checklists.* Washington, D.C.: Home Builder Press, National Association of Home Builders, 1998.

Mitchmen, Ronald D. *Lifestyle Market Segmentation.* New York: Praeger, 1991.

Morgan, Carol M., and Doran J. Levy. *Segmenting the Mature Market: Identifying, Targeting and Reaching America's Diverse, Booming Senior Markets.* Chicago: Probus Publishing Company, 1993.

Parker David F. "Be Ready For The New Retirees." *Building Trends* (August & September, 1996): 6–7.

Piirto, Rebecca. *Beyond Mind Games: The Marketing Power of Psychographics.* Ithaca, N.Y.: American Demographics Press, 1991.

"Planning For Profit: Targeting Specific Consumer Groups Is the Key." *Florida Homebuilder* (July/August 1997): 59.

Popcorn, Faith. *The Popcorn Report.* New York: Doubleday, 1991.

Reid, Lee, E. *Marketing Made Easy: Basics For Home Builders.* Washington, D.C.: Home Builder Press, 1995.

Ries, Al, and Jack Trout. *Marketing Warfare.* New York: McGraw-Hill, 1986.

Schultz, Don E., William A. Robinson, and Lisa A. Petrison. *Sales Promotion Essentials: The 10 Basic Sales Promotion Techniques. . . And How To Use Them.* 2nd ed. Lincolnwood, IL: NTC Business Books, 1994.

Stone, Dave. *New Home Marketing.* Chicago: Longman Financial Services Publishing, 1989.

Thomas, Scott G. *Where To Make Money: A Rating Guide To Opportunities In America's Metro Areas.* Buffalo, NY: Prometheus Books, 1993.

Weinstein, Art. *Market Segmentation.* Chicago: Probus Publishing Company, 1994.

Wellner, Alison S. *Americans At Play: Demographics of Outdoor Recreation & Travel.* Ithaca, NY: New Strategist Publications, Inc. 1997.

Wolfe, David B. *Serving the Ageless Market: Strategies for Selling to the Fifty-Plus Market.* New York: McGraw-Hill, Inc., 1990.

Yntema, Sharon, ed. *Americans 55 and Older: A Changing Market.* Ithaca, NY: New Strategist Publications, Inc., 1997.

A

Launch Campaign Organizer

	Lead Weeks	Weeks To Complete	Start Date	Finish Date	Responsibility
			Stage 1		
Development Team Selection					
Phase I Team	36	3			
Marketing & Sales Consultant Land Planner Landscape Architect Building Architect Interior Merchandiser					
Phase II Team	24	5			
PR/Promotion Agency Advertising Agency Graphics Designer					
Research					
Marketing Feasibility	33	10			
Competitive Analysis Consumer Profile Target Markets Product Positioning Qtrly /Annual Objectives Product Profile Product Mix					
Product Definition					
Site Analysis	33	6			
Site Plan	27	4			
Product Design	24	4			
Product Interior Design	24	6			
Community Name	22	1			

Stage 2

	Lead Weeks	Weeks To Complete	Start Date	Finish Date	Responsibility
Product Definition					
Community Entry	18	6			
Community Amenities	18	6			
Pricing	18	2			
Base Prices					
Premium Prices					
Option Prices					
Marketing & Sales Plan & Budget	18	6			
Inquiry Objectives					
Per Inquiry Costs					
Community Theme					
Advertising Strategy					
PR/Promotion Strategy					
Merchandising Strategy					
Models selection					
Sell Costs					
Budget Revenue					
Budget Expenditures					
Cash Flow					
Public Relations/Promotions	18				
Creative Concepts					
Program Outline					
Program Budget Approval					
Image Creation	18	6			
Logo Creation					
Community Stationery Design					
Business Card Design					
Image Package Production					
Advertising					
Creative Concepts	18	3			
Media Program	15	3			
Media Budget Approval					
Community Merchandising					
Information Center Design	15	3			
Info.Center Display Design	15	3			
Lifestyle					
Comm/Neighborhood Locator					
Site Plan					
Builder/Developer Story					
Floorplans and Elevations					
Interior Merchandising					
Model Interior Design	1816				
Model Names	182				

| | Stage 3 | | | | |
	Lead Weeks	Weeks To Complete	Start Date	Finish Date	Responsibility
Public Relations					
Publicity Production	12	6			
Photography					
Press Kit					
Press Release					
Advertising					
Media Contrats	12	3			
Ad Production	12	8			
Newspaper					
Magazine					
Radio/TV					
Billboard					
Other Directional					
Direct Mail					
Community Merchandising					
Info. Ctr. Display Production	12	8			
Community Entry	12	8			
Walls/Features/Fencing					
Community ID					
On-Site Signage	12	8			
Signage Design/Colors					
Temporary Site Signs					
Traffic Directionals					
Model ID (if required)					
Future Construction ID					
Amenities/Facilities					
Info Center ID & Hours					
Collaterals	12	8			
Marketing Brochure/Cover					
Inserts/Copy					
Elevation/Floorplan					
Map/Directions					
Site Plan					
Community Amenities					
Features/Options					
Builder/Developer Story					
Response Brochure/Cards					
Printing and Delivery					
Landscaping	12	9			
Landscape Design					
Landscape Installation					
Interior Merchandising					
Model Interior Production	12	8			

B

Demographic Data Providers

Leading United States demographic data providers are listed below in alphabetic order.

CACI Marketing Systems
1100 N. Glebe Road
Arlington, VA 232201
(800) 292-2224 FAX: (703) 243-6272
www.demographics.caci.com

Claritas
1525 Wilson Blvd., Ste. 1000
Arlington, VA 22209-2411
(800) 234-5973 or (703) 812-2700
www.claritas.com

Market Statistics
633 Third Avenue
New York, NY 10017
(212) 984-2292 Fax: (212) 983-1533
E-mail: N50@aol.com

National Decision Systems
5375 Mira Sorrento Place, Suite 400
San Diego, CA 92121
(800) 866-6510 or (619) 622-0800
Fax: (619) 550-5800
www.natdecsys.com

For more books that will help you increase sales, check out these titles from Home Builder Press...

Sales and Marketing Checklists for Profit-Driven Home Builders
By Jan Mitchell

This book covers the steps you need to take to create a marketing plan, budget for marketing, conduct basic local marketing research, manage salespeople, develop a system for managing prospects, run a public relations campaign, and conduct promotional events. It includes the major steps involved in the process of selling through the close, the comprehensive selling contract, the move-in, warranty service, and asking for referrals.

Marketing Made Easy! Basics for Home Builders
By E. Lee Reid

Written just for small-volume builders, this book shows how to evaluate your current marketing efforts, determine your cash needs, create a distinct market identity, outline your goals, plan and budget for marketing, and evaluate your competition. You'll also get descriptions of inexpensive marketing ideas and activities that are easy to organize and do. Checklists, forms, photographs, and other examples will help you get started promoting your business right away!

Building Better Ads: New Home Advertising That Works
By Richard Elkman

This popular book provides new ideas on creative advertising strategies for medium and small-volume builders. It explains the ins and outs of advertising, including how to write and design an ad, and why you need flexibility. Also included is information on how to comply with the advertising requirements of the Fair Housing Act. These sections and Advertising Success Stories are liberally illustrated with successful ads, including some classified display ads. Check out the winners of the National Sales and Marketing Awards in the final section.

To place an order or for more information, contact:

Home Builder Bookstore
National Association of Home Builders
1201 15th Street, NW
Washington, DC 20005-2800
(800) 223-2665
www.builderbooks.com